MONUMENTAL LEGACY

THE RISE AND FALL OF
HAMBURG, SOUTH CAROLINA

BARBARA SEABORN

With Foreword by Michael Austin Graybill

MONUMENTAL LEGACY
THE RISE AND FALL OF HAMBURG, SOUTH CAROLINA

iUniverse books may be ordered through booksellers or by contacting:

iUniverse
1663 Liberty Drive
Bloomington, IN 47403
www.iuniverse.com
844-349-9409

Because of the dynamic nature of the internet, any web addresses or links contained in this book may have changed since publication and may no longer be valid. The views expressed in this work are solely those of the author and do not necessarily reflect the views of the publisher, and the publisher hereby disclaims any responsibility for them.

Any people depicted in stock imagery provided by Getty Images are models, and such images are being used for illustrative purposes only. Certain stock imagery © Getty Images.

Scripture taken from the King James Version of the Bible.

ISBN: 978-1-6632-0593-3 (sc)
ISBN: 978-1-6632-0594-0 (e)

Print information available on the last page.

iUniverse rev. date: 09/30/2021

To those who knew the Hamburg story longer and better than I did, shared their knowledge, and trusted me to put this story in book form—in other words, to most of the names listed in the acknowledgments section, a few pages away.

Illustrations

CONTENTS

FOREWORD

As a longtime resident of North Augusta, a city on the South Carolina side of the Savannah River, I once owned land along the river, which I ultimately sold to the River Club Golf Course. During the title search on this property, I was intrigued by the plats and references to what was once the town of Hamburg, South Carolina, and to its founder, a German immigrant named Henry Shultz.

This town grew and survived with lots of varied personality, died nearly a century later in a massive flood, and left a great deal of history in between. Today my home is in the Hammond's Ferry subdivision of North Augusta, where the main street is Railroad Avenue, the very road that once ran through the heart of Hamburg.

For a number of years, I lived across the river in Columbia County, Georgia, a suburb of the city of Augusta. There I met Barbara Seaborn while I was chairman of the Columbia County Commission in the 1990s and she was a writer for the *Columbia County News-Times*. During that time, the board commissioned her to write a book about the history of Columbia County, which was published under the title *As Long as the Rivers Run*. She proved to be a great writer and historian.

Though I moved back to North Augusta, our paths continued to cross. I met with her again, told her of my interest in Hamburg, and asked whether she would be interested in writing a history of that town, its founder, its people, and its final demise. I agreed to underwrite the cost of researching and publishing the book, and Barbara began her task.

After six years of meticulous research, she has breathed life into this story about the little town of Hamburg. Like a newborn baby, the history begins with its founder, Henry Shultz, and from there the town evolves. As it grew, things happened, some good and some not so good. There were trains, barges, and bridges, along with an abundance of people, stories, and events. Finally, Hamburg was on life support when a Savannah River flood destroyed the town.

Barbara Seaborn has captured the pulse of this nineteenth-century town, and although it is a factual history, it reads like a novel. I hope you enjoy it.

—Michael Graybill

PREFACE

Every town has its lore, and Hamburg, South Carolina, was no exception. Besides plenty of local business and industry, the bustling waterfront town became both a market for upstate farmers who brought their crops to sell or ship downriver, and a shopping haven for supplies unavailable to them in their smaller rural towns. Accomplishments of historic proportion by the town or its enterprising founder also happened there, to include a major role in bringing the railroad to South Carolina and the building of the first durable bridge across the Savannah River.

But, as with all places where humans dwell, at least part of what we thought we knew about Hamburg may not really be what happened there. Realizing a certain long-held tradition could not be verified reminded me of another tradition—my own. That's when the Hamburg story became personal for me.

Every family has its lore, and from the time I knew my maiden name was Carver, I also knew about the most famous person in my ancestral past. We were descendants of John Carver—*the* John Carver, who not only came to America on the *Mayflower* in 1620 but also helped organize and fund the expedition. By the time the Pilgrims settled in Plymouth, Massachusetts, John Carver was their first governor. My, I was proud, especially in the fall of the year, when I astonished my classmates with the news that I had a personal connection to the Pilgrims and the first Thanksgiving.

The years may have tempered my childish pride, but when Nathaniel Philbrick's Viking Press book *Mayflower* was published in 2006, I used this opportunity to learn more about my famous ancestor.

Yes, John Carver was a family man—twice. Born in England in 1576, John married his first wife, Mary, when he was nearly thirty years old, and in 1609 the couple had a little girl, who died shortly after birth. Soon, perhaps from the effects of childbirth, Mary also died. John then moved to Holland, joined a Puritan congregation who had fled religious persecution in England, and married his second wife, Katherine. In 1617, Katherine gave birth to John's second child, another girl, who also died in infancy. Three years later, John and Katherine, along with five servants but no children, boarded the *Mayflower* for America.

Following a two-month journey and a harsh winter—which claimed the lives of many, including all but one of his servants—John was doing his own manual labor on top of governing the new settlement. In early April 1621, while he and others were preparing their fields for planting, John complained of a pain in his head, went home to rest, lapsed into a coma, and died. Obviously, as Philbrick and I conclude, John Carver did not have any surviving children. I share this personal experience not to elicit sympathy for my burst bubble but for its similarity to part of the Hamburg story. Somewhere in our past, the little girl and the small town each had a long-held belief that turned out not to be true.

Yes, Hamburg was a real town in a real place along the South Carolina side of the Savannah River, and the town's founder did indeed establish a prosperous trading center to rival neighboring Augusta, Georgia, with whom he had become more than a little displeased. But in time, following a series of circumstances, including the death of that founder and Augusta's recovery of her lost trade, Hamburg suffered what we might call its first fall—though not for long.

After the Civil War, the nearly empty town filled again when it became the new home for several hundred freed Black slaves.

Another phenomenal rise ensued until something happened in this part of the still recovering postwar South that, a little more than a decade later, diminished the town once more.

The War between the States may have been over, but the battle between the races, heightened by a political rivalry that also ran along racial lines, had just begun. Finally, prior to the election of 1876, that dual rivalry erupted into a deadly encounter with far more casualties on one side than the other. In the years that followed, according to oral tradition, the side with the most casualties also received the most blame.

Recently, a number of historians and a few descendants of people from the former town listened to still available family and community lore, combed through printed records, and questioned that long-held belief. A few years ago, some of those inquiring minds asked me to join their research and add what they had just learned to the book they knew I was writing about Hamburg.

I don't think I've ever had a greater challenge or wanted to honor a request more. We agree that this part of the Hamburg story isn't pretty, meaning the account of what happened is basically true. But as new details have come to light on the matter of blame, it's been rewarding to observe how this backward glance is affecting both sides. For those whose ancestors were mischaracterized for so long, there is a sense of appreciation and peace, while there also is an emerging acceptance by the others, who realize many of those passed-down reports were more likely a reflection of postwar thinking and times than an accurate account of what really happened.

While the major part of the Hamburg story can be verified, where I have been presented with any controversial point I have done my best to weigh the evidence, seek multiple sources and advice, and pattern the results after the biblical example of "grace and truth"

(John 1:14). There is no need to trumpet new blame, but only, as much as possible, to set the record straight.

And, dear reader, a request: Since most people with any knowledge of Hamburg at all have only heard about this controversial part, please don't jump to that latter section of the book first. Start at the beginning, and learn why the nearly forgotten town of Hamburg, South Carolina, deserves its "monumental legacy" designation.

ACKNOWLEDGMENTS

As I've discovered throughout my writing years, King Solomon was correct when he said, "The words of the wise are like goads" (meaning the prods shepherds might use to move their sheep along) and, in a second statement, "Of the making of books there is no end" (Ecclesiastes 12:11–12). Thankfully, there seemed to be "no end" to just such persons or resources whenever I needed information, or a prod, to see this book through to its conclusion. Therefore, to local residents who know the area better than I do, and to writers, historians, and all who either shared their knowledge, granted permission to use portions of their gathered or printed work, or in countless other ways encouraged me to write this book, my thanks to you. I offer my thanks specifically to the people listed below.

Michael Graybill is a friend and former colleague from when we were telling the story of Columbia County, Georgia, some years ago, and he was the first to ask whether I would consider writing this book. I'm grateful for his confidence in me and for his patience, advice, and financial support as we worked together again to tell not only this historic story but, in many ways, his own. Besides formerly owning additional parcels of the town's land, Michael now lives in that part of North Augusta once called Hamburg.

Milledge Murray is a newer friend; a descendant of Dr. J. H. Murray, who lived in the original town; and probably the person most knowledgeable about Hamburg of anyone I've met. Though Milledge has spent years researching his heritage, he has been a strong supporter of my brief efforts to tell the story he knows so well. Thanks to his leadership role in the Heritage Council's Hamburg Exhibit in 2012, he also has supplied illustrations and granted permission to research and quote from the reams of Hamburg information still on file at the Arts and Heritage Center in North Augusta.

Peter Hughes is a local historian whose prior fascination with Hamburg resulted in mounds of information he either wrote himself or collected from other sources and offered for my use. I wish I had been here some years back, when Peter occasionally dressed up as Hamburg founder Henry Shultz and shared his knowledge of the town from "personal experience."

Don Rhodes is the *Augusta Chronicle's* prolific columnist and storyteller, who often supplied needed bits of information and kindly allowed me to glean from his portions of the Hamburg story already in print.

Dr. Hubert Van Tuyll, a professor of history at Augusta University, guided me through my second history book and, according to him, changed my apologetic "I'm just a writer, not a historian" into "You are now."

Andrea Spano, a volunteer at the Arts and Heritage Center of North Augusta, where I conducted much of my early research, always seemed to know either the answer to my question or the drawer or bookcase of their well-stocked records room in which the information could be found.

Tonya Guy, the director of the Old Edgefield District Genealogical Society Library assisted me in researching Hamburg's early history, when the town's location was still part of Edgefield County, South Carolina.

Brenda Baratto, former executive director of the Aiken County Historical Museum, provided additional details and illustrations of the Hamburg story. After she had access to the town's updated information, Brenda was also among the planners of the March 6, 2016, event, when both a standing marker and memorial stone honoring all eight persons killed in the 1876 Hamburg massacre were unveiled.

Lauren Virgo worked on the 2012 Hamburg Exhibit at the North Augusta Arts and Heritage Center and followed Brenda as executive director of the Aiken County Historical Museum. Lauren has continued with the Hamburg Virtual Tour project, an online presentation of Hamburg's updated history begun during Brenda's tenure, which is now available to interested South Carolina schools and other individuals.

Nancy Glaser, executive director of the Augusta Museum of History, helped through research, assistance in acquiring materials, and offering an invitation to present my book at a public meeting upon completion.

Larry Lynn, owner of Allegra Printing in Martinez, Georgia, gave his time and expertise in preparing photos, including the cover painting, for publication.

Bruce Wilson, a well-known area photographer, took many of the photos for the book, adjusted others, and transmitted the entire package to the publisher.

Wayne O'Bryant is a descendant of the second group of people to call Hamburg home and is highly knowledgeable about that portion of the town's history. Wayne is most interested in creating a Hamburg district and perhaps a museum on Barton Road in North Augusta, where some of the former buildings from the ruined portion of the original town were relocated or rebuilt.

Reverend Alexander Pope Jr., pastor of First Providence Baptist Church, along with Wayne O'Bryant, supplied information about both the church and the more recent years of Hamburg history. Rev. Pope and fellow church members are also helping to plan that future Hamburg district and museum.

Mayor Robert Pettit, along with the North Augusta City Council and a select committee, has studied the portion of Hamburg history concerning the controversial Meriwether Monument in the city's Calhoun Park and is guiding both the discussion and future use of the monument as an educational tool for the city.

Stephen Budiansky, author of the 2008 book *The Bloody Shirt: Terror After Appomattox*, is an indispensable source of information on the racial and political upheaval in Hamburg and other southern cities during Reconstruction. Mr. Budiansky was present for the unveiling of the new Hamburg marker and memorial stone in 2016. He and his publisher, Viking Press, have also given me permission to quote from his work.

Jenny Heckel is a Clemson University Graduate School student whose 2016 thesis, *Remembering Meriwether: White Carolinian Manipulation of the Memory of the Hamburg Massacre of 1876*, was an invaluable resource for understanding how McKie Meriwether could have been the only casualty of the Hamburg massacre to be honored at the time in such a monumental way.

Anne Sawyer is a longtime friend whose recent death prevents me from thanking her in person for the constant arrival of mail in which she enclosed whatever information about Hamburg she found or had recently been published in area newspapers and other publications.

Frank Christian provided permission to copy the Bernard Willingham painting he commissioned as part of a series of area historic scenes, first displayed at First Bank of Augusta in 2007, for the cover of this book.

Martha Claire Farmer provided information on the old Hamburg Railroad Depot, which her husband, Gordon, restored and placed on the grounds of the family's Augusta Concrete Block Company, located in the section of North Augusta that used to be called "Upper Hamburg."

Finally, the friends and fellow worshippers at my two North Augusta churches, Grace United Methodist and North Augusta Southern Methodist, offered prayers and encouragement that added immeasurably to the prods that helped me reach my Hamburg story destination.

INTRODUCTION

Imagine the good fortune early settlers of southeastern America must have felt when they discovered the mighty Savannah River. Not only did such an abundance of water offer sustenance and economic enterprise, but the river also served as a major highway for boat traffic, the principal mode of travel and cargo transportation at the time. Think, too, of the river's geographic location, providing a natural boundary between the later states of South Carolina and Georgia—unless, through tainted motives or other forms of human ill will, that boundary should become a barrier. Such is the origin of the nineteenth-century town of Hamburg, South Carolina, which became part of the city of North Augusta nearly a century after its birth.

We marvel at the genius of the man who conceived and led the rapid settling of the town, but we decry the injustice that birthed his plans. We also long for a truce that might have brought peace to the man and less upheaval to others who left former homes for the advantages they also believed the new town offered them.

Some of those others arrive midway through our story, when the primary purpose and population of the town dramatically change. The founder has died, and circumstances from local issues to the all-encompassing Civil War intervene. Though the rapidly rising town will not fall completely for nearly fifty more years, another set of tainted motives and new forms of human ill will, unfortunately, remain.

Still, this is a beneficial story, not only for those whose ancestors may have lived in Hamburg but also for anyone hearing about this nineteenth-century town during the early years of century twenty-one. Sadly, and perhaps unavoidably, the old adage "history repeats itself" may spring to our minds and lips as we wonder how such cultural, racial, or political forms of human ill will could have returned to our towns and nation all these many years later.

However, as with a multitude of historic examples, may we learn from this story clues for avoiding similar pitfalls while en route to our new, or hopefully restored, promised lands.

CHAPTER 1

Before the Story Begins

The Europeans were running out of room. Growing populations in small neighboring nations crowded against each other like weeds in an untended garden, and land for expansion was scarce. They also were an adventurous people, unafraid to journey into the unknown, especially if they thought some kind of bounty lay at the end of a far-flung rainbow. Above all, the Europeans were zealous for a cause. Preserving national honor, competing with rival nations for greater wealth and landholdings, and seeking new territory in which to practice their politics or religion were reasons enough to sail across the sea to what was rapidly becoming known as the "New World."

Early explorers of the fifteenth to seventeenth centuries included Christopher Columbus, who, though mistaken about his destination, landed on the southern coast of that New World under the flag and blessing of Spain; Captain John Smith, who planted the seed of Virginia, the first English colony, on American soil; and, in 1620, a group of religious freedom seekers called "Puritans," who founded the first settlement in the future colony of Massachusetts. Grants and treaties between England, Spain, and those who wished to join their countrymen in the New World continued throughout the seventeenth century. In 1663, and of particular interest to our story, England's King Charles II granted a stretch of land between Virginia and Spanish Florida to eight friends who had supported his return to the throne following the tumultuous reign and death of Oliver Cromwell. These friends called themselves "Lords Proprietors" and named their new land "Carolina." In 1670, a new treaty recognized England's claims to all land adjoining the Atlantic coast from Massachusetts to "Charles Town" (later called "Charleston"), Carolina's largest settlement and the namesake of the beneficent king. Six decades later, the Carolina territory was returned to the Crown and divided into two royal colonies. Following American independence, it has been known to this day as the states of North and South Carolina.

For many reasons, Charleston was ideal for attracting settlers to the original Carolina territory. Foremost was the city's wide, safe harbor for incoming ships and, especially for northern colonists moving south, a warmer climate and longer growing season than they had known before. Soil that adapted well for growing indigo, rice, and long-staple cotton was another advantage, as was the abundance of slave labor to aid in producing those crops. Because of this viable combination, plantations soon dotted the landscape, and South Carolina became known as the wealthiest of all British colonies.

In most early settlements along the Atlantic seaboard, the coastal areas were established first, followed by further inland migration as the population and need for land and resources increased. But plantation owners had additional needs. Not only did they require a market for their crops, but they were consumers too. Enter now the need for more trade—a necessary and quickly growing industry in the early American southeast. Next, reconsider the importance of the Savannah River and her tributaries, and we can understand why trading centers began springing up along those inland waterways.

By the middle of the eighteenth century, Augusta was the primary trading center on the Georgia side of the river, while the early towns of Fort Moore and Savannah Town, later combined and called New Windsor, served a similar purpose on the Carolina side.

As the decades continued, the growing number of upriver farmers increased the need for trading centers in that area too.

Now add the arrival of the enterprising German immigrant Henry Shultz, a man with gleams of wealth and opportunity in his eyes and a huge chip on his shoulder, and we have the germ of another beginning: a new and thriving trading center on the Carolina side of the river, which he named "Hamburg" after the German city he had left behind.

CHAPTER 2

𝔚ho 𝔚as Henry Shultz, and 𝔚hat 𝔚as He Doing in America?

The year 1776 was a momentous year for the thirteen British colonies in America. The same could be said for a family living near the city of Hamburg, Germany, a continent away. On July 4 of that year, American representatives to the Continental Congress in Philadelphia declared their independence from Great Britain and birthed a nation. Three months later, the man who would later birth a new town in one of those former colonies was born into that German family.

Most records agree about what Henry Shultz accomplished once he arrived in America but offer little information about his early life, except that he was given a choice between death or leaving Germany after his release from prison following the Napoleonic Wars of the early nineteenth century. Apparently the emperor wanted to make sure this young man never again fought against France.

With much similarity but with some additional details, a recently discovered 1965 article by German author Irene Voigt-Lassen tells of a man named Klaus Hinrich Klahn, who had the same birth date as that of Henry Shultz, while offering credible evidence that these two names are for the same person.[1]

The reader may ask, "Why bring up this disparity at all, since we are most interested in the connection between Henry Shultz and the town of Hamburg, South Carolina?" But some of the later mysteries we've always had about this man, alternately described in superlatives or in less flattering ways, may better be understood if we now interject these plausible, though formerly unknown, details.

According to Voight-Lassen, Klahn—or Shultz—did much more in the first thirty years of life than grow up and fight for his country against Napoleon. Even as a young man, he displayed some of the same work ethic and business skill he would become known for in America. Taking his cue from the extensive North German cattle industry, he established a shipping business for the primary purpose of transporting grain products between planters, who needed seed and other farming supplies, and the dairy or beef farmers, who purchased the harvested grain. He appears to have been quite successful, amassing an impressive amount of property at the same time.

But when Napoleon began his rampage for economic domination across Europe, many businesses were forced to close, Klahn's shipping company among them. With the loss of income plus the debt he had amassed during his business endeavors, Klahn was soon at the mercy of his creditors. The unfortunate man still may have been forced to leave Germany because of his military activity, although some believe his Napoleon story to be an exaggeration. But his indebtedness provided an added urgency for him to go elsewhere. Thus, it appears, Klahn then changed his name to Henry Shultz and became a stowaway on a boat leaving for America. This, we can assume, is how and why he arrived in Georgia in 1806.

However, here we have a definite discrepancy. Many early accounts have Shultz arriving in Augusta in 1806, but that information appears to be in error. It seems more likely that he settled first near Brunswick in southeast Georgia, where he secured work with a pole boat company making regular cargo runs to nearby Savannah and on to Augusta.[2]

Common labor, however, was not his style in Germany; nor would it be for long in America. Right away he developed a frugal lifestyle, saved his money, and soon was able to purchase his own pole boat. It wouldn't be long before he owned more boats. Now the laborer was back in business for himself.

But as he operated his pole boat company, Shultz noticed difficulties in waterborne travel between some of the towns and locales in the Brunswick area. That's when the man with a knack for both problem-solving and grandiose ideas proposed building a canal between the Altamaha River and two nearby tidal rivers to make those connections more accessible. Although his suggestion was initially well-received, the Georgia Legislature was slow to act on the proposal, leading him to consider another idea: changing his address. This is likely why, in 1809, Henry Shultz moved to Augusta, the city he had visited often during those pole boat journeys during the previous three years. Perhaps he could build his new, big-dream American life and industry there.

CHAPTER 3

Augusta, Here I Come

With pole boats in tow, Henry Schultz followed his customary river route through Savannah to Augusta, this time to call the northern city his home—at least for the next decade. For seven of those years, his boats would continue to transport produce and other staples from Augusta to Savannah and would return with manufactured items arriving in that coastal Georgia city from northern ports or Europe.

But managing his pole boat business was only one way our enterprising Mr. Shultz would spend his years and energy in Augusta. Much like the canal he wanted to build in Brunswick, other ideas for improving conditions in his new community—and his own coffers— would soon be underway.

We must be careful to note that during this time, from his arrival in Brunswick through his stay in Augusta, Shultz was a faithful ally of the State of Georgia. Even as he was shipping goods to and from Augusta, when he noticed the amount of cargo leaving the South Carolina side of the river en route to that state's primary port in Charleston, his idea machine flourished again. If only there were a bridge across the river at Augusta, much of that trade could be transported by wagon to the Georgia side and redirected to Savannah. What if he turned this idea into building that very bridge?

Whether from the river's unpredictable depths altering as much as thirty feet between flooding and drought, or because of inferior materials or design, no prior bridge across the Savannah River had ever survived long after it was constructed. For example, floods had already destroyed two bridges built by wealthy South Carolina planter Wade Hampton—the first in 1791, and the second soon after it, too, was in place.

By now it was 1813, four years after Schultz arrived in Augusta, and it was time for him to act on his new idea. First, he would need someone with sufficient experience, likely an idea man like himself, to become his partner in constructing the desired bridge. He found just such a man in the highly regarded builder-mechanic Lewis Cooper. Shultz had the concept, start-up financing and slaves for labor while, from design to completion, Cooper would know how to see the project through. More importantly, Cooper had some idea why those earlier bridges failed.

Reading this story in the twenty-first century, we likely imagine a massive iron bridge such as we often see spanning rivers today. But iron bridges had not yet come to America in the early 1800s. Even thirty to forty years later, when the first ones did appear, they were located in Pennsylvania or the New England states. Thus, from supporting piles to the surfaces, walls, and often coverings, most bridges, at least in the South, were made entirely of wood.

Wood? What kind of wood? Herein lies the difference between bridges such as those built by Wade Hampton and the one the knowledgeable Lewis Cooper—and mastermind Henry Shultz— would soon bring to life.

To determine the age of a tree, we've been taught since childhood to count the rings on the surface of its stump or log. Supposedly, each space between those circular dark lines represents one year of the tree's life. But the rings also tell us something else. A wider space between the rings indicates the tree was fast-growing, while the closer the rings are together, the slower the tree grew. Why does this matter?

Forestry experts explain that the slower-growing trees are not only more durable while alive but also remain so in the timber they provide when cut down for use. On the other hand, faster-growing trees are more susceptible to weather and pest damage while still standing, and to deterioration or rot when their wood becomes timber. For example, the ever popular and available southern pines and cedars are fast-growing trees.

So what does a southern bridge builder do when surrounded by a sea of fast-growing trees but he needs something more durable for his important task? He locates an also common southern swamp and selects a tree that grows there—most likely the slow-growing, top-of-the-durability-chart cypress. That is why, in September 1813, Henry Shultz and eighty slaves traveled to southern Georgia to begin harvesting this valuable timber for his bridge.

Like the natural habitat for the trees themselves, the piles supporting the bridge would be partially submerged in water. Therefore, like the cypress trees, the piles, too, would be resistant to deterioration from weather, insect, rot, and the biggest spoiler of all, the water itself. The crossed trusses forming the sides of the bridge would also be made of cypress, even though the surface, carefully positioned for that maximum flood range of thirty feet above low water, could safely be constructed of nearby, accessible pine. The strength of the cypress timber also meant there was no need to cover the bridge. In retrospect, it seems correct to assume that Wade Hampton and his bridge-building peers were unaware of this important wood-type distinction and built their structures out of readily available pine.

In addition to acquiring timber and other building materials, Shultz and Cooper had further decisions to make. First, they had to determine where the bridge would be built. Then they would need ownership or permission to use the property where each end of the structure touched land. Finally, they needed approval from both Georgia and South Carolina before they could collect tolls from those who would eventually use the bridge. Clearly, in addition to the reason for the bridge in the first place, the tolls were businessman Shultz's plan to pay himself back for the cost of the bridge and, of course, to profit from his grand idea.

In a decision with significance to the present day, the site chosen for the bridge was where Augusta's Fifth Street Bridge crosses the river today. That both ends of the proposed bridge could then adjoin land already in use as ferry landings may also have been a factor in this particular location. On the Georgia side, that landing was near St. Paul's Church, on the original site of the Academy of Richmond County. Shultz and Cooper agreed to pay the academy trustees $400 per year for the use of their land. On the South Carolina side, they were able to contract with Edward Rowel and Walter Leigh to purchase their privately owned ferry landing for $8,500.[3]

Concerning the necessary toll-bridge permissions, they received a charter from the State of South Carolina in December 1813, well before the bridge was constructed, allowing them to collect future tolls for everything that passed over it. Georgia's permission would be granted nearly a year later, on November 9, 1814.

Records are sparse about how long it took to construct the bridge once the timber had been transported to the bridge site. But we do know that Shultz and crew began harvesting the trees in September 1813, and the first toll was received the following July 1, the day the bridge opened. May we also assume there were accolades all around for this enormous accomplishment having been achieved in about ten months' time?

However, for reasons unknown, soon after the bridge was built and before it opened for business, Lewis Cooper sold his interest in their bridge company to Augusta merchant John McKinne. Possibly, there could have been a falling out in his relationship with Shultz, although Cooper's decision may also have been made for personal reasons. Sadly, the only record we have of the bridge builder after this time is the notice of his death just three years after the bridge was completed. His obituary reads in part, "DIED, on Sunday last, Mr. LEWIS COOPER. He was an ingenious mechanic, and the principal architect who constructed the bridge which now proudly ornaments our river."[4]

Cooper was buried in St. Paul's Episcopal Church cemetery in Augusta, beneath a headstone with this touching message: "In veneration of his Character and as a tribute of Respect to his Memory, this Stone is erected by his disconsolate Widow and surviving Children, to mark the spot where lie the Remains of LEWIS COOPER, a Native of Newark, New Jersey, who died September 28, 1817; aged 32 years."

But the bridge, nearly four hundred yards long from shore to shore, and alternately called Augusta Bridge, Shultz Bridge, Hamburg Bridge, or just plain City Bridge, far outlived both its builder and the man who originated the idea. Though weakened occasionally from the river's continued treachery, by the time a raging flood damaged the bridge beyond any possibility of repair in 1888, the structure had served its two-state communities for almost seventy-five years, and Henry Shultz had been dead thirty-seven years.

CHAPTER 4

Profiting from the Bridge and Moving On

The bridge was an immediate success. Traders and their wagons, residents on horseback or in carriage, and foot traffic and accompanying livestock all began using this new access route across the river and paying for the privilege with the following tolls:

- wagon and team, or four-wheeled carriage 75¢
- two-wheeled carriage 37½¢
- rolling hogshead 25¢
- rider and horse 12½¢
- Person on foot 6¼¢
- cattle 6½¢
- hog, sheep, or goat 4¢[5]

It wouldn't be long now, Henry Shultz must have thought, before his popular brain child repaid its entire $73,600 construction cost.

But Shultz and his new partner, John McKinne, were doing far more than counting their profits. As usual, Shultz's mind was full of ideas on how to profit from the bridge beyond the fares collected from its use—with one idea in particular being at the forefront. Had he been a man of caution, he might have exercised patience and opened a bank savings account. Instead Henry Shultz opened a bank.

That's right. In 1816, just two years after the bridge opened, Shultz and McKinne opened their Bridge Bank, housing it in an elegant new building at the corner of Broad and Center Streets near the Augusta entrance to the bridge. How could they afford to take on such a large new project so soon? First, by offering the bridge and other property valued at $105,000 as security, they were able to obtain financing for the bank. Then, in a rare practice still in operation by local groups and corporations today, when the bank proved as popular as the bridge, they issued their own currency. Before long, based on anticipated earnings from both bridge and bank, increasing numbers of Shultz-McKinne "bridge bills" began circulating throughout the area.

We may wonder here whether it wasn't a little soon even for the impressive Henry Shultz to enter such a large new venture while still indebted to the former one. Isn't it also possible that, despite his successes, banking was not his forte? Ah, but his partner was in the banking business already. John McKinne, in addition to owning several local businesses, served as a board member of the Bank of the State of Georgia, the very institution where they had secured their own bank financing. On the other hand, even if McKinne did urge caution, he could have been swept up by the enthusiasm of his partner plus the rapid success of their joint endeavors. Otherwise, at least he might have been more careful in how the bank was organized, especially when currency was involved. Ordinarily there would have been a more thorough record of such an undertaking beyond primarily oral agreements, which seems to be what happened in this case. And in addition to haste and missing records, there also was no customary third-party trustee chosen for what was considered a legal trust.[6] But if McKinne showed any hesitation, it's easy to conclude that the spontaneous, and by all accounts successful, Mr. Shultz may have either discounted these details or told his partner they would attend to such matters later. Right now, the multitasking Henry Shultz had other things on his mind—more ways to circulate those bridge bills for his and John McKinne's advantage.

CHAPTER 5

Better Boats and a Bigger Wharf

Lack of direct access between waterways may have been a problem near the coast, but as already noted, upstream the river itself could be highly unpredictable. Whether from floods following heavy rains or low water levels during a drought, the river often became too dangerous for pole boats to travel there. Now add a new and more obvious problem. As trade and cargo volume increased, pole boats were just too small and too slow. Fortunately, both for Savannah River traffic and for Henry Schultz, modernization of the boating industry at the beginning of the nineteenth century was perfectly timed.

When considering steam-powered engines, our first thought may be of a railroad locomotive. Not so in 1817, when the primary "roadway" for transporting people and trade was still the river. But from London, Scotland, and the United States, inventors spent years adapting the existing steam engine concept from machinery to boats. At first these exploratory boats were far too expensive to build, or so cumbersome their speed was little faster than the pole boats they were designed to replace. This was true of an early steamboat built by Augusta inventor William Longstreet. By 1807, however, a Pennsylvanian named Robert Fulton successfully launched his steamboat, the *Clermont,* on the Hudson River. Meanwhile in the southeast, others adapted Longstreet's idea into a more efficient steam-powered engine until, within the next decade, their steamboats began moving along the Savannah River.

People were astonished by these new boats. Why, they could travel as fast as five miles per hour. How unlike the pole boats, which took several days to travel the distance from Augusta to Savannah, and even longer for the boatmen to row against the current or, likely, carry their boats and walk part of the way back to Augusta.

Dr. Edward Cashin, in his book *The Story of Augusta*, tells of "the excited crowd gathered on Shultz Bridge to watch the arrival of the first local steamboat, *Enterprise*, as it rounded the sand bar, moving majestically at three miles an hour, and towing a barge loaded with 3,000 bushels of salt."[7] Yes, sometimes the steamboats would sail alone carrying cargo and even passengers, while more often they literally were the "engine" that towed one or more smaller boats full of cotton bales or other produce to their destination.

Henry Shultz saw the trend and had another idea. If these larger boats made stops in Augusta, and he knew they could not maneuver the river above the rapids north of the city, they would need a larger docking facility than the small sixty-foot wharf the city had constructed just two years before. His solution? Leasing two riverfront tracts from the city and spending $60,000 of his own funds to build a gigantic six-hundred-foot wharf near the Georgia end of the bridge to serve the needs of these larger boats.

When the wharf was finished, and likely in exchange for its use, Shultz became one of thirty-two incorporators of the Georgia Steamboat Company, to whom the legislature granted exclusive rights to steamboat traffic on all rivers in the state. Along with his new steamboat involvement, he also was named one of seven commissioners to supervise channel improvements in that still precarious upper part of the Savannah River valley between Augusta and Petersburg.

By now the busy, project-oriented Henry Shultz was certainly a man to be noticed. At least, he was no longer called "that poor Dutchman," a term of derision once coined for a man too poor to provide a dowry for his new bride, and adopted by those who scoffed at his grandiose schemes. This was often true when he first arrived in America alone, with empty pockets, speaking little English, and exhibiting other signs of poverty. But now, through persistence, self-determination, and proven accomplishments, by some reports Henry Shultz was considered one of the most outstanding businessmen in Augusta.[8] But to what grandiose idea would he turn his attention next?

Henry Shultz was an enigma. Was he married? Did he have children, hobbies, other interests, friends? Comb the record at this point in his story and you will find very little personal information. One report does mention that his prominence caused "envy and resentment to spring up against him."[9] We shouldn't be surprised at such an attitude, especially by those whose sixty-foot wharf or similar work now seemed but child's play in comparison to his achievements.

But if those dozen years since Henry Shultz arrived in America and nine years of one accomplishment after another in Augusta leave unanswered questions, nothing compares to the mystery that was about to unfold. Here he is at the top of his game, still a young man in his early forties, and he announces he's ready to retire. By his own estimate, he has accomplished enough, far more than he expected to do in America, and he wants to go home to Germany.

And leave all this behind? Apparently so. As local writer Edith Bell Love concludes, "No one ever learned the reason from this strange man."[10]

CHAPTER 6

Dividing the spoils and Preparing to Go Home

Moving was simple for Henry Shultz when he left Brunswick, Georgia, to make that journey north to Augusta. His possessions then amounted to little more than a few pole boats and some personal effects he could easily fit inside. Now his property included at least a bank building, a wharf, and a four-hundred-yard-long bridge. Besides the real estate, he also enjoyed part ownership in several businesses, specifically the Bridge Company, the Bridge Bank, and the Steamboat Company of Georgia. Obviously, he couldn't pack all that onto a ship to take him across the ocean. But as with his past operations, the idea man Shultz already had his divestiture plans in mind.

First, regarding his business ventures, he sold his interest in the Bridge Company, the Bridge Bank, and other holdings to Barna McKinne, brother of his partner, John McKinne. These merchants, well-known both to the Augusta community and to Shultz, seemed the logical choice to add the Shultz enterprise to their own. The agreed-upon price for these entities included Barna McKinne's assumption of Shultz's $63,000 debt, and a personal bond of $500,000 from both McKinnes to protect him from any loss encountered by those circulating Bridge Bank bills. But because the wharf proved too expensive for any one person or group to purchase outright, Shultz established a wharf stock company and sold enough shares to recover the $60,000 the structure had cost him to build.

For reasons unknown, or circumstances beyond his control, all these arrangements took more time than expected. There is also some speculation, based on our more recent information regarding his early life in Germany, that maybe his long-ago debts there still had not been satisfied and he needed to settle those claims before reentering the country. Otherwise, Henry Shultz might have departed for Germany before what happened next on this side of the Atlantic. Called "the Panic of 1819," and still identified as the country's first major depression, the bottom fell out of the surging American economy, including Augusta, Georgia, and the perpetual good luck charm surrounding Henry Shultz suddenly disappeared.

Hardest hit were the banks. A combination of excessive speculation in public lands and poor banking practices, including the unrestrained issue of paper money beyond the nation's reserves to redeem them, caused many banks across the country to fail. On May 24 of the same year, owing to a demand for specie on its nearly half million dollars in circulation, the Bridge Bank was also forced to close. Quite possibly, thinking back to that agreement John McKinne and Shultz had made to organize the bank and circulate their own currency, their bank was yet another participant in those prevalent poor banking practices in vogue at the time.

But hadn't Henry Shultz already divested his interest in the bank to the McKinnes? Yes, but without Shultz's knowledge, by this time the McKinnes had borrowed much of that circulating currency to shore up their own sagging companies.

Knowing the McKinnes' bond now could not protect him from financial responsibility, Shultz dropped his plans to leave the country, reentered the firm, and invested $15,000 of his own funds to help satisfy that obligation to the Bridge Bank. But it was too little, too late.

Unfortunately, besides drawing on the bank bills, the McKinnes had also mortgaged the bridge along with other property to the Bank of the State of Georgia; this was the very security Shultz and John McKinne had used to build the Bridge Bank building in the first place. Less than two years later, the Georgia bank foreclosed on the mortgage.

Everything Henry Shultz had spent the previous decade to achieve was gone. He was a ruined man, a disillusioned man, an angry man. Surprisingly, his anger was directed not at the McKinnes but at the Georgia bank, who he was convinced had other, fairer options to consider than foreclosure. He also maintained that, as the bank should have known, the mortgage itself was illegal. With the bridge used as security both to build the bank and to issue the bridge bills, how could it also offer enough security for that additional McKinne mortgage?

Needless to say, Henry Shultz did not return to Germany. Instead, with the same determination that propelled him to success just a few years before, he began a fight to regain his losses from the moment he reentered the firm. That fight, primarily with the Georgia bank, would be full of unforeseen twists and turns and would linger for the rest of his life. However, in typical Henry Shultz style, despite depleted finances, newer and still grandiose projects would continue to be the core of his life. This time, larger than a bridge, a wharf, or even a bank, his next project would be a town—Hamburg, South Carolina, namesake of the German city he had once before called home.

But first, in the following chapter, we'll slow the momentum and explore some of this devastated man's attempts to regain financial solvency and respectability amid some missteps of his own.

CHAPTER 7

In Defense of Henry Shultz

From the record of those intervening two years between the panic of 1819 and foreclosure of the McKinne mortgage in 1821, it seems clear that injustice indeed had been served by the Georgia bank in its dealings with Henry Shultz, and to some extent with the McKinnes. In the following financial summary, comparing bridge cost, income, and profitability with what the McKinnes had already repaid on the mortgage, it's difficult not to conclude that part of the responsibility for the loss of the bridge belonged to the bank. In retrospect, who could blame Henry Shultz for protesting such a dire consequence, especially when almost none of the missteps at the time were his?

- initial cost of the bridge: $73,600
- income from bridge tolls, 1815–1821: $85,656
- McKinne mortgage on the bridge: $90,000
- McKinne property already sold to satisfy the mortgage:
  o Warehouses: $30,000
  o Slaves: $40,000
- Balance on the mortgage at foreclosure: $20,000[11]

Besides the relatively low balance still owed when the bank foreclosed and took control of the bridge, was there no consideration that just two years' worth of tolls would have paid off the rest of the mortgage? Also, within the next decade, or before the bank sold the bridge to Savannah businessman Gazaway Lamar, the bank would realize more than ten times the value of the bridge in tolls.

Thus, according to popular opinion, and not just that of Mr. Shultz, it does appear that the Bank of the State of Georgia enriched itself with little thought for what those profits had cost Henry Shultz. Surely he shouldn't have been obligated to give them that much return on a much smaller mortgage.

Henry Shultz fought hard. Still, at one point, following successive lawsuits, protests, and ineffective pleas for resolution, he was so despondent he attempted suicide. But his method—placing a loaded pistol in his mouth, angled upward toward his brain—did not succeed. Instead, by some movement or miracle, the bullet struck between his eyes and exited through his forehead with no loss of brain function or sight. However, for the rest of his life, Henry Shultz bore the scar where the bullet emerged, leading many to describe him as having "the mark of Cain" on his forehead, based on the biblical story of Cain and Abel in Genesis 4:15.

In addition to his actions, either by continuing pleas to the bank for justice, or for sympathy from the public, Shultz often expressed his feelings about the terrible crisis that had befallen him. Since he fought this battle for the rest of his life, or about the next thirty years, the following examples of those outbursts are not necessarily in chronological order.

> It is to me that Augusta owes the main public enterprise she boasts; monuments not less of my toil than of her injustice, my honest and laborious gains were snatched from my hands. I was stripped, not only of my hard earnings, but of my last and dearest possession—my good name. I was cast out, stigmatized and broken. The people of Augusta treated me with the blackest ingratitude, while I was acting the part of a faithful servant for them. They made me a victim of persecution ...

> If a man, of an unbiased mind and with only common sense can be found in Augusta who knows the facts, ask him, and he will tell you that justice will restore the bridge to its proper owners, as sure as the sun will rise tomorrow morning.[12]
>
> My words and deeds have sustained me before the bar of Justice, and my words and deeds shall sustain me before the world. But, if the actors of the Bank of the State of Georgia at Augusta look upon their acts and deeds in this affair, they will look upon their eternal disgrace before God and man. Signed, Henry Shultz.[13]

Now we shall resume the narrative of Shultz's newest idea: building that town across the river, both to rival Augusta and to exact revenge for the treatment he received there. Now it's not just the Georgia bank he detests but also the Georgia city and the State of Georgia, from which he will intentionally divert trade away from that state's primary port of Savannah, and redirect it toward the port of Charleston in South Carolina.

CHAPTER 8

Henry Shultz Begins Again—Again

If he could build a bridge, a wharf, and a superior reputation for ability and accomplishment, he may have asked himself, "How much harder could it be to build a town?"

But if there is one thing we shall learn about Henry Shultz, as perhaps with all presumed geniuses, it is that even the most brilliant among them have gaps in their knowledge or expertise. It was true Henry Shultz had bigger ideas and larger dreams than most people do, and a matching supply of energy and determination to bring them to fruition. What he did not always have were the subtitles pertaining to what to do next, in what order, or when. And, as we have seen before, one such lack that arises over and over, both in his Augusta and soon-to-be Hamburg years, is the patience to finish—and pay for—one project before beginning another.

Although we might not agree with his motive for building what has been called, among other unflattering names, "a spite town," the trading center on the opposite side of the Savannah River would become a boon for farmers and traders not only in South Carolina but also from as far away as North Carolina and Tennessee. The fortunes of many were made or increased after Henry Shultz created the new town of Hamburg.

While pondering the exact location of his new town, Shultz may have thought back to the time he first noticed large numbers of boats arriving at and leaving the South Carolina side of the river. That sight spawned the idea for his bridge, primarily to draw the trade in those boats from South Carolina to Georgia. Now, thinking in reverse and desiring to remove that trade *from* Georgia, he gazed across the river again.

What he noticed this time was a spacious cornfield lining the level portion of the riverbank, reaching back nearly a quarter mile to an impressive fifty- to seventy-five-foot foot bluff rising behind. The level part of the land, he envisioned, would provide more than enough room for the business section of the town, while homes with breathtaking views and protection from the ravages of river flooding could be built along and above the bluff. He also knew the river's current was stronger there than on the Georgia side, which meant the river channel would be deeper, making it easier for steamboats to dock at the new wharves he also would build there.

But there was more. Besides the practical reasons for choosing this location, the South Carolina side also offered superior health considerations. Since the level portion of the riverfront was two to three feet higher than on the Georgia side, the land would be dryer there than in Augusta, even when flooding was not a factor. Yes, like Augusta, the land was still swampy in places, but this swamp would be intentionally drained before any building on the site began. Finally, Shultz knew there were four springs near the bluff to provide all the safe, fresh water needed for future residents of the town.

Now, just as he and Lewis Cooper needed to secure the property where their bridge touched land, Henry Shultz had to find out who owned that cornfield. As it happened, one couple were the sole proprietors of that 330-acre tract he felt would be sufficient, at least for the initial phase of the town.

Known as "the Fair tract," the cornfield had been owned for a long time by Isaac Fair and his second wife, Lucilla. But following Isaac's death and Lucilla's marriage to John Covington, the new couple became guardians of the property for the rightful heirs, Isaac Fair's minor children. Thus the land was not for sale, but it could be leased.

This is how, on June 6, 1821, in an arrangement that was in vogue at the time, the Covingtons could enter into a contract to lease those 330 acres to Henry Shultz for a period of six years, at the price of $500 per year. During that time, Shultz agreed to drain the swamp, lay off lots and streets, build warehouses, erect wharves, and lease lots to others for the purpose of building their own commercial buildings or homes. At the end of the lease, Shultz would be given the option to purchase one fourth of the improvements made on the property upon payment of a proportionate value of the land they occupied, at the estimated price of $7,000. The rest of the land, including improvements, would then revert to the former owners, assumed to be the Covingtons or, perhaps by then, the grown Fair children.[14] With those necessary property matters out of the way, nothing else prohibited Henry Shultz from getting to work on his big, new project. Now, even before a lot had been cleared, a nail hammered into board, or a prospect found for one of those eventual homes or commercial establishments, all these considerations must have been just the elixir Henry Shultz needed to cross that bridge he still called his own, to where he would live for the rest of his life.

CHAPTER 9

Hamburg, Here I Come

Anyone familiar with the origin of the Town of Hamburg has likely read something like this: "A tradition grew up about Hamburg that, in just one night, and by a single proprietor, the fronts of several houses were erected. ... and within two months, about 100 houses were all inhabited by an industrious population."[15] Oral traditions die hard, or perhaps some ambitious fiction writer was only attempting to see his sensational work in print. That "single proprietor" was, of course, Henry Shultz, about whom many fictitious accounts, as well as correct reporting, would be written throughout his colorful career. Tradition has it that the fronts of a few houses were erected in one night, presumably to attract the consternation of Augusta onlookers from across the river, but the rest of what supposedly happened within two months' time cannot be substantiated. However, as beginnings go, what actually occurred in early Hamburg history is almost as unbelievable as the fiction.

As nearly as we can tell, on July 2, 1821, barely one month after signing his lease with the Covingtons, Henry Shultz began the construction of Hamburg. And, in roughly half the time it took to complete his bridge, by December of that year the town did indeed have enough houses for the forty-four families and about two hundred people who already lived there.

Did Shultz do this all by himself, with financing from that Georgia bank? Hardly. We may be speculating here, but we do know he had help from friends, some of whom may have given him a place to stay until he could build his own home. Also, he or they would have had slaves to do much of the construction. Concerning financing, he could have had some savings left from the stock sale of his wharf, plus whatever cash remained after he sold out to return to Germany. Perhaps, too, he was able to prelease some of those lots and buildings before they were completed. Remember: these were still basically colonial times, when pioneers or new settlers mustered the sheer grit to eke out their livelihoods by themselves or in partnership with each other.

However, if there was one assistant Henry Shultz did not need, it was someone to advertise his accomplishments and praise him for what he had done. He could handle that task all by himself, and he did. Near the end of 1821, as the initial layout of the town was nearing completion, he composed a lengthy account of what was already built, available, or still planned for his new town, and he submitted it to every known South Carolina newspaper, as well as to the *Augusta Chronicle* and *Savannah Republican* in Georgia. Along with his submission he included a message to each editor that once they had printed his information three times, they could send proof of such to him and receive payment—presumably because his summary was, after all, a full-blown advertisement inviting others to live and do business in Hamburg. The following is a portion of that summary, nuanced now and then with reminders of Hamburg's superiority to Augusta.

> The undersigned announces to the public that he did commence, on July 2nd last, to erect a town named Hamburg in South Carolina, opposite Augusta on the Savannah River and, with the assistance of friends, to build 78 buildings, which include a 50 x 300 foot warehouse for cotton and tobacco, a 50 x 70 foot public house, and a number of spacious stores calculated for different types of businesses.

All these buildings are 2–3 feet above the level of the streets in Augusta and will be safe from damage due to floods. Already 2,500 bales of cotton have been stored in the warehouse and goods have been sold in proportion. There is also a spacious building calculated for a church. Between the buildings is a 150-foot wide street intended for a market street.

There is also a good, safe boat landing, and substantial wharves will soon be erected for loading and unloading. More warehouses will be built, all with good drainage, free from danger of fire, and with storage prices about half the rates charged in Augusta. There is also a Post Office, which will open two hours earlier and be kept open two hours later than the one in Augusta for the convenience of merchants. About a quarter mile from the river the ground elevates some 60 feet, affording handsome and healthy situations for residence, and on which are a number of springs of as good water as this country affords.

As Hamburg will attract citizens of South Carolina, North Carolina, and Tennessee, and nature having done much for it, if assisted by art, the undersigned has not the smallest doubt it will become a place of great importance.

—Henry Shultz[16]

His advertising worked. Almost immediately, Shultz reported that 1,083 bales of cotton had been received in Hamburg in just one week. Before long, as word spread throughout his target audience, cotton bales would be only a portion of the goods bought, stored, or sold in the fast-growing new trading town of Hamburg.

But soon, no matter with whom or at what cost he had begun this project, after that initial spurt, or about the end of the first year, Henry Shultz really was out of funds. Yet once again, as with the invention of the steamboat, both for him and for the State of South

Carolina, the timing couldn't have been better. Shultz's new idea? Convincing the leaders of the state that the new town of Hamburg could be as profitable for them as, with their help, he expected it to be for himself.

CHAPTER 10

Georgia and South Carolina: Neighbors, but Not Always Friends

The rivalry between Shultz and Augusta was not the first time competition over land, trade, and economic prosperity between Georgia and South Carolina had occurred. Although the primary reason for establishing the later Georgia Colony had been to provide a buffer for British interests in the New World against continued encroachment by the Spanish and the French, that buffering soon took on an added purpose.

James Oglethorpe, the acknowledged founder of Georgia, and his fellow Georgia trustees advertised their colony in superlatives. "A New Eden," they called it, this combination haven for England's poor; resource for raising profitable silk, rice, and cotton for the mother country; and oasis of social purity where, in their minds, the other colonies had failed. In theory, this purity would occur through a set of prohibitions, especially against slaves and rum, which were thought to be detrimental to the work ethic necessary for settling their new land. Of course, it didn't help that neighboring Carolina had no such prohibitions.

Carolina's perspective had been in place for years. Almost as soon as Englishmen began settling on the eastern side of the Savannah River, savvy settlers joined the Spanish, French, and prior English colonists in the lucrative business of Indian trade, even if that meant trespassing beyond their own territorial limits and crossing into land still held by the Indians.

At first the Indians carried their deer skins and beaver pelts to the traders at the primary transportation site, the river. In return, the traders dazzled the Indians with guns, rum, blankets, and an array of trinkets that lured them easily into their plans. Soon, however, the traders were not only meeting the Indians on the western side of the river and on their land but were also indulging in such dishonest practices as incorrect weights and other forms of unfair trade. If only James Oglethorpe had let things be, the traders might have prospered indefinitely with their mercenary upper hand.

The Georgia founder had several concerns about conditions in what was called the Back Country, as opposed to the Low Country near Charleston and Savannah. How the Indians were being treated was one of them. The French, and to some degree the Spanish, were still lurking by the edges of both colonies, and Oglethorpe knew it was to England's advantage to treat the Indians well, lest they turn to those who benefited them the most. Whoever gained the allegiance of the Indians and controlled the Indian trade, all three governments knew, would eventually control the much-desired Indian land.

Already lauded for his diplomacy with the Indians, Oglethorpe secured an amendment to the original treaty, which had allowed the first Georgia settlement in Savannah, in order to establish a new trading post in the Back Country, called Augusta. Regardless of the stated reason for this decision, both sides knew it was, in fact, an attempt to keep the Carolina traders honest.[17]

Now fast-forward to the nineteenth century. Although the states of Georgia and South Carolina were well past their origins, with the aid of a wronged man's efforts to regain South Carolina's upper hand over Georgia, that rivalry continued.

The Savannah River may have belonged to both states since early settlement days, but what traveled up and down that mighty stream had been up for grabs ever since the first cotton fields and other products of enterprise began appearing on both sides. Furthermore, competition for the lucrative import-export business between the two major seaports, Georgia's Savannah and South Carolina's Charleston, was equally fierce. Knowing all this, a confident Henry Shultz made the short journey to the state capitol in Columbia to discuss the future of Hamburg with the South Carolina Legislature.

CHAPTER 11

A New Partnership for a New Town

Let's pause for a moment to consider the irony of what is about to happen. The South Carolina trading and shipping business, which had climbed to new heights just a few years before, began to slow after completion of a bridge across the Savannah River built by none other than Henry Shultz. Those wagonloads of produce that once stopped at Savannah Town or Fort Moore for shipment downriver to Charleston were now crossing the Shultz bridge for the very purpose of transferring that wealth to Georgia. And the bridge builder himself wanted to reverse that course?

But Henry Shultz was no stranger to the legislators or to the Charleston businessmen who, at the same time, were suffering financially because of that slowdown in their port city. His own business reputation, the number and magnitude of his achievements, preceded his visit. They knew about his bridge and bank problems, but they believed his partners and their dealings with the Georgia bank were the real culprits in that financial dilemma, not he. Also, they were very much aware of what he had begun to do in their state and wanted to hear more about his plans for Hamburg.

What an opening for his sales pitch. Did the legislators realize that by restoring direct trade between Hamburg and Charleston, the state would regain the estimated $2,000,000 per year in storage and shipping fees from upper Carolina and neighboring states that was currently going to Savannah and the State of Georgia? What he needed from them to make this idea possible, he explained, was

33

a loan of $50,000: $35,000 for additional buildings, wharves, and warehouses to enlarge the town, and $15,000 for a steamboat to transport that trade to and from Charleston. He also requested a five-year tax exemption for all town property, facilities, and professions. Last, and with allusions to his Augusta experience, he asked that a bank be established in Hamburg "to protect the inhabitants against the rivalry and opposition of those institutions in Augusta."[18]

The legislators were most receptive to his presentation. Following a brief but appropriate discussion, they granted his requests, with the exception of the bank. Terms of the loan included a six percent interest rate for a period of five years, with security to be approved by a board of five commissioners. In return, Shultz was to give the commission his personal bond for $100,000, secured by his one-fourth interest in the Fair tract plus the improvements thereon.

True to form, Henry Shultz lost no time in putting his workmen, his newly acquired financial resources, and himself to work.

CHAPTER 12

Location, Location, Location

From the founding of Carolina to the Revolutionary War, the colony was subdivided into districts, and for nearly a century before the emergence of the town of Hamburg, this particular part of Carolina was called the Edgefield District, after her largest settlement of the same name. In 1785, when the new state divided her districts into counties, Edgefield became the name of the area's new county, and its largest town the county seat. But the town of Edgefield had one drawback. There was no large body of water, no source for long-distance transportation, nearby. Hamburg might never become the largest town in the county, but it would not be long before the new riverfront trading center outstripped her county seat in nearly every other way.

How well Henry Shultz understood that the advantage a large body of water held for his town. Long before the trip to Columbia or even his choice for the location of Hamburg, he had been part of the Georgia commission to improve navigation along the shallower areas of the river. Now, thinking of his own transport, and knowing that even the expansive Savannah River did not flow directly from Hamburg to Charleston, he had another project in mind.

Combining his work on the navigation commission with that once unfulfilled plan for similar water travel improvement between Brunswick and Savannah, he now saw the benefit of widening and deepening sections of the coastal waterways connecting the Savannah River with Charleston. With the advent of steamboats, he realized how much safer and faster travel between the two destinations could be with a less dangerous and more direct route than the roundabout passage available at the time.

Henry Shultz was on a roll. Fresh from his successful acquisition of funds from the state legislature for Hamburg, when he requested additional monies from the City Council of Charleston for better navigation near their city, they were more than happy to comply. With sentiment running high for the project, the council allocated $20,000 for those very improvements around sea islands, inlets, and other impediments between the city and the Savannah River. But, with even more excitement for the improved economic activity in their city, they had further ideas—and an open purse to match. Anticipating overland traffic between Charleston and Hamburg as well as by water, they set aside still more funds for two roads to be built from Hamburg, one each to intersect with existing roads to Columbia and Charleston.

Meanwhile, even before water travel improvement plans were attempted, Henry Shultz used the $15,000 portion of his state loan to purchase the steamboat *Commerce*, and to begin making those roundabout trips to Charleston. True to form, he announced proudly that he had made the initial one-way journey in only five days, one day less than it took the Georgia Steamboat Company's boats to travel from Augusta to Savannah.

CHAPTER 13

Hamburg: Growing, Growing, Growing

By the fall of 1823, scarcely two years after changing the name of the Fair tract cornfield to Hamburg, and little more than a year following his visit to Columbia for state help, Henry Shultz sent what must have been an eye-popping report to the legislators with a list of what had been accomplished in the town they had helped build. As unbelievable as it may have seemed, this report was indeed fact, not fiction.

Hamburg now boasted 176 buildings, including 114 private dwellings, 39 stores, 4 public houses, 2 warehouses, 2 physician's offices, 2 blacksmiths, and one each of the following: church, post office, school, printing office, market house, druggist's store, silversmith, butcher's house, tailor, saddler, painter, and its own weekly newspaper, the *Hamburg Gazette*. All this and more, he claimed, served an estimated population of eight hundred to one thousand residents.[19]

But no matter the massive buildup, the fast-growing population, or even the astonishing twenty-four thousand bales of cotton passing through the town in less than a year's time—or perhaps because of it—not everyone was happy with this successful new trading center.

From the beginning, Augustans had scoffed at Henry Shultz and his pretentious idea for a new town, but they weren't scoffing now. Instead, along with their equally concerned counterparts in Savannah, residents of the long presumed most important trading center along the Savannah River knew they had to do something to regain, or at least slow, the pace of their vanishing trade. Though this process would take time, these are some of the steps they considered.

First, since one of the reasons up-country farmers began stopping in Hamburg to ship their goods downriver was to avoid paying tolls to cross the bridge into Augusta, the city secured a temporary agreement with proprietors of the bridge to allow wagons full of produce going to or from Augusta to travel toll-free, while empty wagons returning to Carolina were still required to pay the toll. Other measures included some of the very features Henry Shultz had extolled as the reason Hamburg was superior to Augusta as a trading town. Now not only Augusta but also the Georgia Legislature, from whom they requested aid, promised changes to those features.

Yes, because of the Georgia Steamboat Company's monopoly on Georgia rivers, their steamboat rates were too high. It was also true that at the same time South Carolina legislators were aiding navigation between Hamburg and Charleston by granting loans and waiving taxes, Georgia's leaders were imposing tonnage duties on arriving freight and levying taxes on sales of imported articles in Savannah. Furthermore, because it was difficult for large ships to reach the wharves in Savannah, much of the ocean commerce had been diverted to Charleston.

But one solution depended on the Georgia cotton growers themselves. They could improve the way they harvested, stored, and baled their crops. It was no secret why Georgia cotton was considered inferior to South Carolina cotton. For example, the Georgia growers might hide rocks or place lower-quality cotton in the centers of the bales, weigh when the cotton was damp to make it heavier and more costly to the buyer, cause injury to the crop from careless exposure to weather, and ship or store their cotton in round bales rather than in the preferred squares.[20] In yet another bit of Georgia–Carolina irony, it seems fair to say, those long-ago Carolina traders and their treatment of the Indians had no monopoly on dishonesty.

Although the Georgia Legislature would follow through with most of the above changes through regulation and closer supervision, that wasn't enough to halt Hamburg's continued rise. In time, Augusta would create other, more successful, ways to recover their lost trade. But for now, with increasing activity for storage in the warehouses and transport to Charleston, plus continued growth in population and profit from a growing number of stores and other services, Hamburg's economy seemed destined to go nowhere but up.

So was it time for Henry Shultz to rest at last? Far from it. Based on his town's steady growth, and likely his own overconfidence, even before sending his progress report to the legislature, Mr. Shultz, who seemed to be operating in perpetual motion, decided to purchase an additional 398-acre tract of land above the waterfront level of Hamburg, to more than double the size of the town.

Really? On top of his other debts, was his income sufficient to add the $15,500 cost of this new property, now being sold upon the death of former owner Walter Leigh? Somehow, according to the 1824 Edgefield County Deed Records, Henry Shultz gave a mortgage for the whole purchase price. At the same time, he arranged for another mortgage on this new tract to John Covington, from whom he had leased the Fair tract, and the next year yet a third mortgage for $42,000 to a Mr. William Snowden. The Leigh tract would be known as Upper Hamburg.

But that's not all Henry Shultz stacked on his plate around this time. The state may not have included a bank in the assistance they gave him the previous year, but on July 2, 1824, the third anniversary of the founding of the town, a determined Mr. Shultz announced the opening of the Bank of Hamburg, South Carolina. For bank stock he combined his personal assets with all his interest in the town, and for income he offered loans at seven percent interest for up to two-thirds the value of whatever cotton, tobacco, or other produce the borrower had stored in the warehouses. Almost immediately, in a story that is beginning to sound very familiar, banknotes signed by J. M. Tillman, Cashier, and Henry Shultz, President, were in circulation.

Had "Banker Shultz" learned a lesson from his former Bridge Bank experience? Was Cashier Tillman the missing trustee in that earlier banking venture? Apparently not, for as soon as the bank bills began appearing in Augusta, their value was questioned. Even worse, before the end of the year, the *Augusta Chronicle* and *Georgia Advertiser* reported that this new bank was "in very bad repute" and had, in fact, suspended specie (currency) payment.[21] Despite efforts to operate the bank a while longer, in less than two years those bank notes were declared worthless and the bank itself ceased to exist. It would be another decade before the South Carolina Legislature officially chartered the first stable Bank of Hamburg.

Many glory days and prosperous years lay ahead for the fledgling town of Hamburg, South Carolina. But the failed bank would not be the only bump in the road ahead for Henry Shultz.

CHAPTER 14

Will the Real Henry Shultz Please Stand Up

For the next few years, or during the latter 1820s, the reader may ask, "Are we talking about one person here or two, or even three?" No, just as we've been surprised already by how much Henry Shultz was able to accomplish, perhaps akin to the work of two or three men in such a brief period of time, we'll soon learn that the same often amazing and still productive founder of Hamburg had another, less spectacular, side. Consequently, he did not necessarily leave misfortune behind when he crossed that bridge from Georgia into South Carolina. And when trouble arrives this time, it may be harder to find someone besides himself to blame.

Obviously, by now Henry Shultz has incurred a great deal of debt. There was the original mortgage to the Covingtons for the Fair tract, at least two more for the Upper Hamburg Leigh tract on top of the $50,000 loan from the State of South Carolina, and even more indebtedness to an individual for another $42,000. Also, though his bank may have closed, he was being asked to make restitution for those formerly circulating bank bills. Still, during what might be called his "pay-the-piper" time, Henry Shultz will also reveal an adept ability to meet new challenges and survive ruination, just as he did after losing his bridge and bank on the other side of the river—at least for a while. But when bills came due and Shultz either could not or did not make the payments, others took action too.

The first ax to fall came at the hands of the county sheriff, who announced in January 1825 that a number of his lots in both the Leigh and Fair tracts would be advertised for sale the following March. But with time to spare, Shultz managed to sell fifty lots in Upper Hamburg for a net gain of $37,000, which was enough to satisfy his creditors at the time and forestall the sheriff's announced sale. A similar escape plan for the Fair tract would occur later.

By the next year, with growth nearing two hundred houses, sixty stores, and twelve hundred residents, aside from financial problems for Shultz and attempts from rival Augusta to scale back their competitor's progress, business was booming in the still rising town of Hamburg. In the fall of the year especially, when newly harvested crops were brought to the trading center to sell, store, or ship to markets farther away, those local stores did some heavy business of their own. With hundreds of visitors in town, primarily farmers and their families who now had money for stocking up on necessities, or simply to enjoy the pleasures of a wide variety of goods and opportunities unavailable in their small country towns, Hamburg was a shared treat for buyer and seller alike.

Business was also booming for the building trade. At Shultz's direction, another sturdy wharf was built to meet the needs of at least six steamboats now traveling to and from Charleston, instead of just the single *Commerce* he had purchased with funds from the legislature. About this time, Shultz also allocated some of his energy and resources toward building a fine new home for himself atop that scenic bluff now known as Shultz Hill and surrounding it with gardens and a park for the townspeople to enjoy. Stories are still told of the grand feasts and other gatherings held at that magnificent location, especially the annual Mechanic's Society Festival, held on July 2 of each year, the anniversary of the town's beginning.

Likely a forerunner of today's labor unions, mechanic's societies were prevalent in early nineteenth-century America for a similar purpose: to elevate the status and standard of living for artisans, builders, and other skilled workers in a laboring trade. Monthly meetings had been held almost since the founding of the town, but after Shultz petitioned the legislature for an official sanction for the group in 1824, the annual Mechanic's Society Festival became possibly the town's finest gala of the year. That was certainly true on July 2, 1827, the sixth anniversary of the town, even if this year Shultz's hilltop home wasn't chosen for the eight hundred to one thousand people who were expected to attend. A more accessible lavishly decorated warehouse in town would do just fine.

This event, this society, may have been one of Henry Shultz's best ideas yet. He wasn't the only Hamburg resident who suffered setbacks, or the only person who, from time to time, needed the proverbial shot in the arm. Therefore, besides honoring the town's laboring class, he turned this year's festival into a pep rally for the entire town.

And what a rally it turned out to be.

The day began outside the warehouse with the firing of six guns, one for each of the town's six years, followed by a dramatic welcoming address by host Shultz, who combined highlights from the town's past with his totally positive predictions for the future. Next came the midday procession through two arched house frames, erected for the occasion, and into the enormous warehouse equipped with a row of tables long enough to seat every guest. Officers of the society, dressed in their identifying regalia, were seated at the head table beneath a giant flag inscribed with the society's motto, *"Nil Desperandum,"* meaning "No need to despair."

Then came the bountiful feast, said to be sufficient for all assembled to eat heartily, and had there been one thousand more guests, there would have been enough food for them as well. Finally, the festivities ended with the customary toasts, thirteen in all, honoring everyone and everything connected with the festival: the day, the town, and especially founder Henry Shultz; mechanics and artists, whom they called "Journeymen of the Architect of the Universe"; and various state and national leaders, including Congressman George McDuffie.[22]

By all accounts, the pep rally was a huge success. Not only was the town reinvigorated, ready to press on toward that prosperity Shultz had proclaimed in his welcoming speech, but the founder himself must have fallen asleep that night replaying the toast his grateful town had raised to him earlier in the day: "To Henry Shultz, founder of the Town of Hamburg, whose firm, independent and manly course, tempered with prudence and talents, enables him this day, triumphantly to behold his favorite offspring, still prosperous and successful; and in him we behold a man who, for its subsequent prosperity, is prepared to risk and, if necessary, to sacrifice his all."[23]

He woke the next morning, July 3, likely contemplating how he could extend the revelry into celebrating the country's beginnings on July 4. And what good, lasting memories this festival would provide for Henry Shultz—especially a little more than a month later, when he found himself in jail.

CHAPTER 15

Henry Shultz: Down but Not Out

The story made headlines in area newspapers for days. A trunk owned by two White women had been stolen, and a nearby Black boy was accused of the crime. No, he didn't do it, the boy protested, until a severe whipping convinced him to make a confession. But it wasn't his idea, he cried. A White man named Joseph Martin made him do it. Though Martin also denied the charge, the authorities didn't believe either story and took them both into custody.

After learning about the incident, Henry Shultz, who by now was also mayor of the town, decided to go to the jail and see whether he could solve the problem. Without accusing either the man or boy of the crime, he began by simply asking Martin if he would help him find the trunk. Whether guilty or not, Martin seemed relieved and agreed to the request. And so the search began. Martin and the boy, Shultz, and two companions set off on a miserable, pouring-rain day to look for the missing trunk.

It was not a pleasant experience. In addition to the weather, Martin kept taking them from one place to another without success until Shultz suspected he was leading them on a wild goose chase. Angry and drenched with rain besides, he and the other men alternately whipped Martin and dunked his head into a ditch full of muddy water. Still no confession. Finally, after the heavily bruised man had swallowed so much water that he fainted, Shultz expressed regret for their actions and ordered the punishing stopped. He then took Martin to his own home and sent for a doctor. But nothing could be done for the injured man. A few days later he was dead.

The trunk was never found, and thus it was never proven that either Martin or the boy was actually a thief. Perhaps even the women's story was false. But however misguided their actions, Shultz and his companions had caused a man's death. All three were convicted of manslaughter and, by mid-August, sentenced to six months in the Edgefield County Jail.

But while in prison and still convinced of Joseph Martin's guilt, a disgruntled Shultz penned the following letter to the editor of the *Augusta Chronicle*: "Let it be remembered that it was for the act of a thief that I have been and now am suffering in a dungeon, for it was his act that produced mine." The editor couldn't resist adding a comment of his own: "Of course, never mind that Henry Shultz took the law into his own hands."[24]

The governor of the state, however, must have been moved by Shultz's self-defense, for he would pardon all three men the following January, several weeks before their sentences were up.

Life went on in the still bustling town of Hamburg even without Mayor Shultz at the helm. In December 1827, the town was officially chartered by the state, becoming the second incorporated town in Edgefield County and, almost from the beginning, earning the title of largest inland trading center in the state. But for Shultz, life was a different story. His town may have been bustling, but by the time he was released from prison, his own affairs were in shambles.

Reenter the sheriff, who, following foreclosure of one of the Leigh tract mortgages, again listed lots in both the Leigh and Fair tracts for sale. With rumblings also from other creditors for repayment, the sheriff made another move: placing Shultz back in prison for insolvency. It may have been too late to recover the Leigh tract, but by agreeing to turn over a large part of the Fair tract property plus other holdings to trustees who, in turn, sold sufficient assets to once again satisfy his creditors, prisoner Shultz was again a free man. But he still wasn't free of debt.

Five years had passed since Shultz requested and easily received that $50,000 loan from the state. Five years—the length of time he had also been given to repay the entire amount, not just the scant portion he had repaid by then. Worse than returning him to prison a second time or putting a lien on the remainder of his personal property, the state now threatened to confiscate his town. However, when Shultz made a counter threat to send all Hamburg's downriver trade to Savannah instead of Charleston, the state realized they were no match for crafty Shultz and withdrew their threat.

But there were other problems, not only for Shultz this time but also for the town and the state. The river was low again, so much so that steamboats had to be deactivated, making pole boats again the sole method of transportation for river traffic.

When adding the slower speed of the smaller boats to the greater distance from Hamburg to Charleston than to Savannah, partly caused by the failure of those plans to improve coastal navigation, most trade now had to be diverted to Savannah after all.

Yet there were still shared positives in both the thriving trade center and for her recovering founder/mayor. Traders still brought their crops to Hamburg and still shopped in the abundance of stores and businesses in the town, and Georgia had taken care of another disadvantage to the formerly rising South Carolina trade by removing those detrimental taxes and import fees in Savannah.

As for Shultz, after noticeable improvement in his financial condition, the state legislature renewed their confidence in him with two momentous moves. First, in 1832, they chartered that long-promised branch of the South Carolina Bank in Hamburg. Then, in early 1833, they forgave the unpaid balance of his $50,000 loan and declared his already repaid amount of $16,225 "paid in full."

Speaking of improvement in Shultz's finances, this might be a good time to clear up something that could be questioned later in our story. Although the early section of Hamburg continued to be known as the Fair tract, neither the circumstances of that initial lease nor any reference to the Fair children appears to be mentioned again. Just as Shultz had continued dealings with the Covingtons when obtaining that extra mortgage for Upper Hamburg, perhaps there also was a family agreement at some point to sell the formerly leased land to Shultz because the Fair children either moved elsewhere or, for other reasons, were not interested in keeping the land. Otherwise, Henry Shultz would not have been free to make further financial transactions with town property, which does continue to occur throughout his tenure in Hamburg.

But now let's go back to what we do know was happening there at this time.

Loan forgiveness for the town's founder wasn't the only significant event for Hamburg, Shultz, or the state in 1833. Business leaders and citizens of the port city of Charleston were hurting. Tired of depending on the water level of the Savannah River for their livelihood, they had been working on an alternate solution for years. The year 1833 was also the year that the long-anticipated railroad reached all the way from Charleston to Hamburg.

CHAPTER 16

All Aboard!

Public rail transportation did not begin in this country or in Europe until well into the nineteenth century. But the railroad concept was in use as early as the 1500s, when European miners discovered it was easier to move their coal or iron ore out of the mines in small, horse-drawn carts along thin wooden rails than for man or beast to carry it to the surface one hod or scuttle at a time.

By the 1700s, English coal-mining companies were also building short wooden railroad tracks above ground, except that the rails were now covered with iron strips. However, as Americans would learn a century later, wooden rails are subject to swelling after a rainstorm and curling in the hot sun. Since these fluctuations plus wear and tear caused the iron strips to separate from the wood, it became necessary to construct the tracks completely of iron and attach them to embedded split logs (ties), the method used worldwide today.

Incidentally, the distance of four feet, eight and a half inches between the original parallel rails corresponded to the length of the average axle connecting the wheels of a horse-drawn wagon—an accommodation to the "engines" that propelled the first trains.

Besides settling the problem of rail composition, attention also turned to something more effective than natural horsepower to move the trains. With steam-powered boats already in operation, railroad pioneers agreed that if steam worked on water, it should work just as well on land. The British were the first to develop a steam locomotive, which by 1825 evolved into the world's first public railroad.

America entered the era of rail transportation in 1830, when the Baltimore & Ohio Railroad Company became the first to offer service in North America. The company's first trains were not powered by steam, however, but with horses aided by wind-powered sails mounted on top of the rail cars. Still, the concept of steam power remained in the minds of many, including inventor Peter Cooper, who developed the small, one-and-one-half-horsepower steam locomotive *Tom Thumb*, which roared to life for an experimental run on Baltimore & Ohio's thirteen-mile tracks later that year.[25]

But even before the Baltimore & Ohio Company launched its first-in-the-nation railroad trains, William Aiken and Alexander Black, two businessmen from Charleston, South Carolina, had already considered the railroad as the solution to both the problem of low water on the Savannah River and, by default, loss of trade to the more accessible shipping port of Savannah. They knew about rail experimentation in England. They also knew that railroad tracks required only half as much space as the wider wooden-plank roads then in use for overland wagon travel. Thus, railroad tracks would be less costly both to construct and to maintain.

Aiken and Black, and by now a growing number of other Charleston business leaders, held many consultations about putting this revolutionary idea into action, even considering how far and along what route these trains should go. Aiken, besides being a friend of Henry Shultz, was very familiar with the town of Hamburg. Of course Hamburg, with its warehouses and prime location along the river, plus its proximity to the city of Augusta, would be the perfect ending point for their railroad.

The state must have agreed, because on December 19, 1827, in response to a proposal by Mr. Black to build and operate just such a railed road, they granted a charter to the Charleston group for the requested Charleston & Hamburg Railroad. A few weeks later, after some concern that the wording of the charter could be too restrictive for potential future projects, the charter was amended to become the South Carolina Canal and Railroad Company, or SCC&RR, with the Charleston & Hamburg Rail Road—C&HRR—being one of the company's operations. William Aiken would become president of the larger company, with Alexander Black at the helm of the railroad project. Though the charter was then potentially more inclusive, the railroad acronym would nearly always be the recognized name of both the project and the company, though there is no evidence that any other undertaking was ever attached to SCC&RR.

CHAPTER 17

𝔚e've 𝔅een 𝔚orking on the 𝔕ailroad

Deciding where the railroad would begin and end was only the tip of the C&HRR iceberg. Many, many decisions about the route, including the lay of the land, types of soil over which the rails would go, plus interaction with existing thoroughfares and population centers, were yet to be made. Timewise, the planning period to build the railroad took place during a few months of 1827 and culminated with the issuing of the final charter in January 1828. But it would be exactly two years from that time, in January 1830, that construction of the railroad would actually begin. The twin challenges of surveying the land and mapping the route claimed nearly all the months of 1828 and 1829.

Surveyors, civil engineers, land developers, and even those Charleston business leaders who doubled as financiers to sell stock in the railroad company to fund the railroad were all indispensable partners in this grand project. But not one of them knew anything about building or operating a railroad. Would Henry Shultz come to the rescue again? Ah, no. Truth be told, the man who had initiated so many building projects in Augusta and Hamburg wasn't even in favor of the railroad. Remember: he owned steamboats. He had built a bridge, wharves, and warehouses, all with river traffic in mind, and certainly the readily available river was a far less expensive "roadway" than even a railroad. Although he would eventually accept the importance of the railroad, even to donating the land on which the Hamburg "depository" (later shortened to "depot") would stand, he was a reluctant Johnny-come-lately to the railroad idea.

But fortune smiled on the Charleston and Hamburg Company in the person of Horatio Allen, a New York native and, according to most sources, the most influential man in railroad circles at the time. An inventor and civil engineer while still in his twenties, Allen became chief engineer for the Delaware & Hudson Canal Company in Pennsylvania, who themselves were just entering the field of railroad experimentation. Although their first trains were powered by the customary horsepower, they were also interested in the new steam engine concept and sent Allen to England with instructions to purchase several steam locomotives for the company.

Allen managed to find just one somewhat crude barrel-boilered machine called the *Stourbridge Lion*, which he had dismantled and shipped back to Pennsylvania, where it was reassembled. This young man made history during the engine's trial runs by becoming the first person to operate a steam-powered locomotive, not just in America but in the Western Hemisphere.[26] However, after further experimentation, the company decided that although the little steam-powered engine could pull the train, it was still inferior to horsepower. So they brought back the horses to power their trains.

Allen did not agree with the D&H Company's decision. Yes, the first steam engines were little more than crude attempts to accomplish their purpose, as was the case with the *Stourbridge Lion*, but he felt they had promise. In a burst of youthful opinion, perhaps, he was heard to say, "There was no reason to believe that the breed of horses would be materially improved, but that the present breed of locomotives was to furnish a power of which no one knew its limit, and which would far exceed its present performances."[27] That is why, in May 1829, shortly after his twenty-seventh birthday, Horatio Allen left the Delaware and Hudson Company, and traveled to Charleston, South Carolina, to talk steam-powered locomotives with officials of the C&HRR.

CHAPTER 18

Corral the Horses; Full Steam Ahead

The men of Charleston needed little convincing either to concentrate on steam locomotion or to hire Horatio Allen as the chief engineer for the new Charleston and Hamburg Railroad. Of course, it would be some time before Allen actually drove a C&HRR train. For now he would use his *civil* engineer training to become chief adviser for mapping the route, laying the tracks, designing and purchasing what ran on those tracks, and anything else connected with the railroad enterprise.

Meanwhile, William Aiken and others were still hard at work on matters of the land and route. All agreed that the Charleston starting point should be at Line Street, an alleyway between King and Meeting Streets some two miles northwest of the city center. From there on, however, alternate surveys were still being conducted and judged against each other for distance and feasibility, and decisions made and remade before the final route could be determined.

From notes taken by the surveyors, they learned where the soil was sandy, supported by firm clay, or "sloppy and very bad." Others counted "six considerable valleys 15 to 20 feet deep and several hundred yards wide, being considerable obstacles to a railway."[28] Alternating with the valleys were the obvious hills, especially a fourteen-mile stretch rising 375 feet in the area of Horse Creek between the future town of Aiken and Hamburg. This area near the ultimate end of the railroad would be difficult to navigate even after the road was complete, and there would be continued improvements made on that section of the tracks until it was permanently set in 1852.

After merging three separate surveys, the length of the railroad was measured at 149½ miles. But there was a fourth survey. After Horatio Allen arrived on the scene, he was able to fine-tune the route over easier topography and reduce the distance near both the Charleston and difficult Horse Creek areas, which culminated in the eventual, and historic, 136-mile length by which the C&HRR has been known ever since.

But it was by no means necessary to wait for the entire route to be settled before the first sections of track were laid, and it was only necessary for a small section to be constructed in order for testing of an actual railroad prototype to begin. You see, Henry Shultz was not the only person who had doubts about the railroad. As we already know, other than foot travel, horses were their primary means for moving person or product from one place to another on land, and the average speed of a horse was about six miles per hour. So when "experts" spread the rumor that if the trains traveled at the projected speed of thirty miles per hour its passengers wouldn't be able to breathe and would all die from suffocation, "testing, testing" was another important prelude to the anticipated C&HRR trains.

The first test took place along 150 feet of experimental track in Charleston, where company officials hitched a small flanged-wheel flatcar filled with cotton bales to a single mule. Spectators were stunned at how easily this small, far from powerful animal pulled its load along the tracks. Though experiments continued, there is no record of the little mule pulling any more railcars, or future naysayers fearing loss of life at such "high-speed" travel.

By the time the first permanent tracks were laid at the beginning of 1830, Horatio Allen had made other improvements besides refining the route. One major decision, likely arrived at after one of the experimental rail cars did tip over on a curve, was to increase the distance between the rails to five feet—about six inches more than the former axle-length apart. The greater distance, he believed, would create better motion stability, whatever the curve, rise and fall of the track, weight of the load, or, most of all, speed.

Allen also made trips to Maryland to compare notes with the Baltimore and Ohio Railroad Company. In addition to learning where best to purchase equipment, he was most interested in checking their progress with steam engines. Although the B&O Railroad Company's experimentation with steam had begun earlier than similar pursuits in South Carolina, by the time the men of Charleston conducted their first official steam-powered railroad run on Christmas Day, 1830, the Baltimore and Ohio was still uncertain whether steam or natural horsepower was the better way to move a train.

CHAPTER 19

The Best Friend of Charleston

Horatio Allen was both convinced and convincing that the matter of steam power was settled. Besides his belief in the basic superiority of steam over horses, with steam there would be no need for stables full of fresh horses at intervals along the route, or food and blacksmiths to keep the animals fed and in condition for their limited-distance runs. In contrast, steam engines could be fueled by scrap wood from the roadside, and steam created from any available water—even contaminated water, which might sicken the horses.

By now the men of Charleston were also convinced it was time to put their steam-powered plans into operation, but it was difficult for them to persuade stockholders to provide funds for an as yet unproven idea. Fortunately, local businessman E. I. Miller was willing to spend the needed $4,000 to buy what would become the first fully operational steam-powered locomotive built in this country, on the condition that if the completed engine proved worthy, the C&HRR would then purchase it from him. (It should be noted here that the Baltimore & Ohio's *Tom Thumb*, built about the same time, was only a prototype and was never put into use.)

Miller consulted the local firm of Eason & Dotterer, makers of heavy machinery, to draw up plans and specifications for a basic design, which he then sent to the West Point Foundry in New York, where the locomotive would be built. A throwback, perhaps, to the long-standing practice of naming horses, all the early steam engines were also given names. Appropriately, from the time construction began on the C&HRR's first steam locomotive in the early summer of 1830, it was known as the *Best Friend of Charleston*.

The *Best Friend of Charleston*, from a sketch
on page 24 of Thomas Fetters's book *The
Charleston & Hamburg* (author's collection).

We can understand the naming custom, but what of the engine's appearance? From early photos, it's difficult to see any resemblance at all to the trains rumbling through our cities and towns today. Without explanation, we would hardly know what to call this stubby little vehicle, which was about the size of a small truck yet had neither exterior walls to hide the tall vertical boiler, nor seat, railing, or other accommodation for the engineer or crew.

However, although steam has now given way to diesel power on our modern trains, Horatio Allen would be proven right; for more than a century, his present breed of locomotives did "furnish a power of which no one knew its limits." (See chapter 17.) And regarding appearance, aside from the necessary changes to our newer engines today, their size, along with that of the entire train, still reminds us of the old "choo-choo" that chugged through our cities, towns, and memories until the middle of the twentieth century.

West Point Foundry completed building *Charleston's Best Friend* in about four months, after which it was disassembled, shipped down the Atlantic coast, and welcomed with great fanfare and newspaper coverage on October 23, 1830. Within days, the men at Eason and Dotterer—including the young, newly-trained member of the crew, Nicholas Darrell—reassembled the *Best Friend* and began making trial runs on the limited set of tracks around Charleston. Excitement grew as success followed success, except for one early-November run. That day, with Darrell as engineer and financier E. I. Miller and several friends on board the single passenger car, just as the train slowed near the end of the run, one of the forward wheels turned inward, causing the engine and passenger car to leave the track.

Fortunately the damage was minimal both to the engine and those on board. Darrell and his fireman sustained only a few bruises, and within weeks the forward wheel had been repaired. Trial runs resumed in early December, culminating on December 14 when the locomotive, pulling two fourteen-foot passenger cars filled with forty men and traveling twenty miles an hour, completed a final and mishap-free run along both directions of the now five-mile track.

At this point, two important decisions were made. First, after stockholders were convinced of the locomotive's worthiness, the C&HRR honored their agreement with Mr. Miller and purchased the *Best Friend* from him. Then, amid further fanfare, on Christmas Eve the Charleston papers announced that on the following day, "The Rail Road Company's new steam-powered locomotive [would] hereafter be constantly employed in the transportation of passengers." Following times of departure and other details, this note appeared at the close of the announcement: "Great punctuality will be observed in the time of starting."[29]

Would any Charlestonian ever forget the Christmas of 1830? At least not the 141 passengers who took that first trip between Line Street Station and the community of Sans Souci, then the end of the C&HRR line, nor the 300 additional passengers who rode the second and third ten-mile round trips later in the day.

News of the historic first steam-powered passenger train in America was reported around the world, including this enthusiastic account written by one of the passengers, a sportscaster known as Jockey of York:

> Away we flew on the wings of the wind at the speed of 15–25 miles per hour, annihilating time and space, and like the renowned John Gilpin, "leaving all the world behind." It was nine minutes, five and one-fourth seconds since we started and we discovered ourselves beyond the forks of the State and Dorchester Roads ... We came to Sans Souci in quick time. Here we stopped, then darted forth like a live rocket, scattering sparks and flames on either side, passed over three saltwater creeks, hop, step, and jump, and landed at Lines (station) before any of us had time to determine whether or not it was prudent to be scared.[30]

CHAPTER 20

Capitalizing on Success; Learning from Failure

The much heralded first excursion of the *Best Friend* was by no means a one-time event advertising some future form of public transportation. No, as announced earlier, Christmas Day of 1830 was the first day of continuous rail service, operating four times a day between Charleston and Sans Souci, and soon carrying freight as well as passengers. On January 15, 1831, the C&HRR arranged one trip especially for their stockholders. Celebration was likely the theme of the day, but the company also used the time to enlighten the group on both the current state of the railroad and plans for the future.

Already several circular sections of track, or turntables, had been added to existing tracks so the engine could be unhooked, turned around, and reconnected to the other end of the train for a return trip on the single track. But as the route lengthened and the company added more trains, rather than construct another complete set of parallel tracks, they added small sections, called turnouts or sidings, at strategic locations to make it possible for two trains, well-timed and going in opposite directions, to safely pass each other. Also, to alleviate lingering fears of a boiler explosion and injury to passengers seated directly behind the engine, a small barrier car loaded with six cotton bales would now be installed between the engine and the passengers for their protection.

But the highlight of the day must have been the agreement between the company and stockholders for a second locomotive to be ordered from the West Point Foundry. Possibly in gratitude for the foundry's share in the success of the *Best Friend*, they named the new engine *West Point*, after them. Some design changes would be made first, most notably that the boiler would no longer be vertical, but horizontal.

Scarcely two months later, the *West Point* arrived in Charleston and, on March 5, 1831, made its initial two-and-a-half-mile trial run around the city with 117 passengers on board. But Eason and Dotterer realized other changes needed to be made before the *West Point* was ready to be put into regular service. Thus, for now, the familiar *Best Friend* would continue to be the only locomotive pulling a C&H train. But sooner than the company or anyone else expected, the status of their primary engine would change.

The next historic first for the *Best Friend* happened on June 17, just six months after that Christmas Day beginning. There were no passenger cars this time, but just the engine, with Nicholas Darrell as engineer, and his fireman, the second person in the now regular two-man crew, who was to keep the fire and steam going while the engineer drove the train.

Their orders were to go up the line, now past Sans Souci, and bring back lumber cars waiting for them at Eight-Mile House. When they arrived at their destination, Darrell told his fireman to turn the engine around while he checked on the lumber cars.

But after the engine was turned, and as he waited for Darrell to return, the fireman became annoyed at the hissing sound made by steam escaping from the boiler. Not being familiar with the equipment or the power of steam, he found that if he held the safety valve down by sitting on it, the hissing would stop—and it did, temporarily.

Suddenly, without warning and with no way to release the increasing pressure inside the boiler, the cylinder holding the boiling water exploded, throwing the badly scalded fireman into the air and tossing him to the ground. With the scalding, plus a broken thigh from the fall, the fireman did not recover and died two days later. This man's death then became the first fatality on an American railroad, and the incident dampened the enthusiasm for the new railroad just six months after it began operation. Also, the explosion all but destroyed the *Best Friend*, ending all activity on the C&HRR for a full month, or until the *West Point* was ready for service in the middle of July.

The news traveled fast throughout the American railroad world and resulted in additional changes to both equipment and its use. While still experimenting with steam power, the Baltimore and Ohio decided there should be two safety valves connected to the boiler, one of which would be out of reach by either the fireman or engineer, and neither of them ever fastened down. The explosion also increased the use of barrier cars between the engine and the rest of the train, and prompted the addition of railings to aid and protect the engine crew.

With the *West Point* now the railroad's only in-service engine, plus a constantly growing demand for both passenger and freight service, the company realized they needed to order yet another locomotive as soon as possible. This replacement vehicle would be larger than the others and would be called the *South Carolina*. After further study, Horatio Allen decided that doubling the number of wheels from four to eight would improve the engine's stability and driving power. Because this action also doubled the engine's size, there now would be room for two boilers instead of one, as long as they reverted to the original, upright position. Such drastic changes, however, meant that the South Carolina would not be ready for service until February 1832, another six months away.

The *West Point* and *South Carolina* then served as the C&HRR's only locomotives for another eight months, until they were joined in October of that year by the *Phoenix*, the company's fourth steam engine. Or was it? Surprisingly, the remains of the *Best Friend* had not been destroyed after all but had been gathered up and taken to Eason and Dotterer, where they were reassembled to more up-to-date specifications and turned into a fully functioning locomotive once again. The name *Phoenix* likely refers to the mythical Greek bird that obtained new life from the ashes of its predecessor.

By this point, the growing and apparently successful C&HRR Company employed four engineers—a sufficient number at least until their engine fleet increased even more. Compliments also must go to the men at Eason and Dotterer. While the West Point Foundry continued to supply information and equipment as needed, the local company's expertise was growing. Within the five-year period from 1830 to 1835, at least seven C&HRR locomotives came out of the Eason and Dotterer shop, including the *Charleston*, the *Constitution*, and the *Hamburg*.

Meanwhile, as the company's fleet and business were expanding, so also was that eventual 136-mile length of track on which the trains were to run, even if not at the same or even desired pace. Progress was especially slow at the beginning of 1831, when the crew averaged only three-quarters of a mile a month. By the end of that year, the track had reached only the community of Woodstock, just fifteen miles from Charleston, or ten miles above Sans Souci, where the *Best Friend* had stopped a full year before.

The delays were understandable. Sometimes the land itself was still a problem, especially patches of quicksand and the ever-present marshland that could not always be avoided or routed around. Labor shortage was another factor, as was the lack of access through the woodlands for transporting workers and obtaining supplies. Those impeding forests, however, proved to be a blessing as well as further cause for delay. In most cases, landowners were happy to donate not only their rights-of-way for the tracks to pass through but also their timber for building the trestle work (ties). Still, it was a long process before those trees became useful timber. After the trees were harvested, the logs had to be taken to a lumberyard, cut to size, dried, and then shipped back up the rail line to the work site.

But when the company turned more of its attention to track building, 1832 became a markedly different year. By February the labor force had risen to thirteen hundred, including slaves hired from local plantations, and by summer the track had reached Summerville, equaling the distance covered during all of 1831. By the end of the year, the C&HRR track was sixty miles long, or nearly half the distance to Hamburg. The year 1833 would be even more spectacular. That was the year the track reached all the way from Charleston to Hamburg and achieved the designation "The Longest Railroad in the World."

CHAPTER 21

The Longest Railroad in the World

Aside from steady progress in laying the remainder of the C&H track in 1833, the thrill of reaching such a historic milestone would not be easy, and it would not be mishap-free. Except for that difficult section at Horse Creek, the track was rarely the problem. The locomotives, still in their early trial-and-error stage for both equipment and design, were.

Near the end of 1832, one of those twin boilers on the *South Carolina* exploded, removing the locomotive from service for several months while the boiler and other repairs were made. By June of 1833, and for want of a new frame and wheels with stronger axles, the *West Point* was sidelined. Now that the trains were becoming longer and heavier, the axles were a frequent problem for all the older models and required much attention from Horatio Allen and his counterparts at Eason and Dotterer to solve.

Following repairs to their existing fleet and the addition of the *Barnwell* and *Edisto*, the C&HRR now had six in-service locomotives, fifty-six freight cars, and eight passenger cars. All this and real estate valued at just over $15,000, plus a 137-mile track, would be impressive enough for a still relatively young company. But the highest honor of all occurred on October 3, 1833, when the C&HRR track finally reached Hamburg and became the longest railroad not only in this country but in the world. A special train carrying South Carolina governor Robert Young Hayne and other state leaders travelled the entire distance from Charleston to Hamburg to commemorate that historic day.

The C&H was also poised to reap an impressive amount of income as well as prestige. With one hundred seventy thousand bales of cotton reaching Augusta and Hamburg each year, and rail freight rates offered at half those charged by wagon or stage, the company expected at least half that amount of cotton would be shipped to Charleston by rail. Adding freight coming the other way, plus fares from an estimated one hundred passengers a day riding the full length of the railroad, C&H anticipated, and apparently earned, their early goal of $453,000 a year.

According to later records, those projections were not only met but exceeded. When service began on the partially completed tracks in 1831, the company earned $58 a day. By the spring of 1833, the daily amount had risen to $120, and by 1835 to $1,000. Newer and more efficient equipment led to still longer and heavier trains, resulting in still more income. Certainly the vision of the men of Charleston only a few years earlier had more than come true.

Testaments to the railroad founders are still evident in the towns and cities that appeared along the rail line. The town of Blackville, the first overnight stop on the new railroad, was named for Alexander Black, the man who had submitted the original request to the state legislature to build the railroad. The next year, 1834, the locomotive *E. I. Miller* was named in honor of the financier who purchased the *Best Friend of Charleston*, the railroad's first steam-powered engine. And in 1835, the new town (later city) of Aiken would be named for the president of the railroad company, William Aiken, though he would not live to learn of the honor. Sadly, even ironically, he was killed in a Charleston carriage accident in May 1831, when his horse was frightened by the noise of an oncoming train.

As for Horatio Allen, the brainpower behind the making of the railroad, the town of Allendale, South Carolina, was named for him, even if he did not choose to live there or in the state much longer. Instead he married Mary Simons of Charleston and left the city in 1835 to travel abroad. Later he resettled in his former home state of New York, where, among other projects, he became the consulting engineer for the Brooklyn Bridge.

CHAPTER 22

All Roads Lead to Hamburg

Not only did Hamburg receive an influx of freight and passenger traffic from the railroad, but more and more traders swarmed into town from already established origins in upstate South Carolina and beyond. More cotton, tobacco, and farm produce arrived either to be stored in the warehouses until sold or to be sent to Charleston by rail. And imagine the thrill of Charleston-bound travelers accustomed to spending two to three days to make the same journey by wagon or stage now being able to board a morning train in Hamburg and reach their destination that afternoon. Yes, the world-famous C&H train added a huge boost to the bustling town of Hamburg, South Carolina—at least for now.

While earlier reports tell of increased traffic and clogged roads on the outskirts of town during harvest season, now such movement must be described in more vivid terms. The new traffic jams could be five to six miles long, moving as slowly as one mile per hour, and lasting for days at a time. And what happened to the farmers, their families, or their crews when night fell? They parked their wagons off the side of the road, unpacked their camping gear, and formed tent cities, likely making close new friends at the same time.

But going to Hamburg was still a highlight of the year for these primarily infrequent travelers. Though the resident population of the town may rarely have exceeded fifteen hundred, about one-third that of Augusta, there was plenty for visitors to do, see, and purchase before returning home. Local merchants spread out their welcome mats and wares, apparently convincing shoppers they did not need to cross that bridge into Augusta to stock up on supplies. The farmers collected most of their earnings at this time of year, and the harvest season was just as profitable for the locals as it was for them.

Grocery stores, clothing outlets, and hardware and specialty shops with the farmers' needs in mind, could all be found there. Livery stables and resident blacksmiths were also on hand to care for any necessity relating to the horses. Then too, the town's bank, post office, legal and medical services, and so forth must have been an added convenience for transacting business whenever these smaller-town folks came to Hamburg.

While most towns of any size today can boast an array of eating establishments, there's no record of fast-food restaurants lining the streets of Hamburg in the 1830s. Quite likely, plenty of picnicking in and around those tent cities satisfied their hunger needs just as well. However, we do know of two newly built hotels where food and overnight lodging could be purchased. But even earlier, at least the men could unwind at L. B. Holloway's Billiard Room, where, besides enjoyment, the owner offered a reward for the return of stolen billiard balls—and even more for conviction of the thief. At the same time, the ladies enjoyed searching the shops for boots, bonnets, fabric, and other delightful goods to brighten their wardrobes and their homes.

In addition to the buildup inside Hamburg, similar to the lengthy process from planning to completion of the railroad, much discussion on how to improve those crude and sometimes impassable dirt roads leading into town took place all during the next decade. Throughout the country, from the mid to late 1800s, better roads were often made of wood, and these were called plank roads.

To construct such a road, builders followed a method similar to that of laying railroad tracks. Logs placed across an average twelve-foot-wide roadway served as the foundation, after which boards eight to twelve feet long were overlaid lengthwise to create the surface. Drainage ditches were then dug along each side to prevent water and mud from rising to the level of the planks and causing the wood to deteriorate. When carefully built, these roads provided safer travel for the horses and a much smoother ride for the wagons, their riders, and their loads. But because of the cost and time required to build these roads, they were not freeways. Thus, tolls became an added cost for the farmers, who might compensate by making their empty-wagon return trips on nearby dirt roads to save that expense.

Once again the little town of Hamburg made history. When their twenty-six-mile stretch between Hamburg and Edgefield was completed, it became the longest plank road in the state at the time. This road also paved the way for today's, many more times upgraded, US Route 25.

Most reports credit Henry Shultz, along with aid and support from his town, for building that historic road. This may have been true at the outset, although the road was not completed until after 1850, and perhaps even after Shultz's death. We should also note that after a few decades, plank roads fell out of favor when, in spite of those drainage ditches, the cost to maintain or replace deteriorating wood was just too cumbersome and too high.

Meanwhile, there is more to tell about the founder of Hamburg during the remaining two decades of his life.

CHAPTER 23

In Defense of Henry Shultz—Again

Despite his now world-famous railroad town, forgiveness of his state loan balance, and other points high and low in the life of Henry Shultz, the loss of his bridge prior to the birth of his town was never far from his mind. He may have tempered his aggression—for example, no longer having to be forcibly removed from the toll booths after the mortgage had been foreclosed—but his attempt to recover what he never stopped believing was rightfully his continued to the end of his life. Through lawsuits by his own efforts and seeking aid from the state legislature and even Congress, he tried repeatedly to right this perceived wrong.

Were there not other matters demanding his attention and time? And what of his later history—the debts he accumulated along with his continued accomplishments? But lest we, as many compilers of the Henry Shultz story have done, dwell mainly on his financial problems, it's important to note that Shultz was not the only Hamburg resident who did not, or could not, always pay his bills. Sometimes he had as much difficulty getting paid for the lots and other properties he sold to someone else as his creditors had in their dealings with him. Yes, he could be unwise in his financial transactions, and his debts were on a larger scale than most. He also may have been the greater target for criticism because of his public stature.

But his accolades were numerous too. Some of the best evidence of this fact took place following a summary of his Hamburg accomplishments, which he delivered to the South Carolina State

Legislature on December 17, 1836. While not as common today perhaps as in the past, such a presentation at the time was called a "memorial" when offered as a written statement of facts or a petition to a legislative body or an executive.

Shultz did indeed write out his lengthy portrayal, which, along with an equally extensive response, can still be read in its entirety at the Arts and Heritage Center of North Augusta, as well as in either the Old Genealogical Society Library housed in the Tompkins Library, or in the nearby Old Genealogical Society Archives in Edgefield. The following are but some of the highlights of that extensive communication.

He began with thanks "for giving to an obscure and friendless foreigner a mark of confidence" when they granted him that $50,000 loan, followed by a recap of his threefold purpose for building the town of Hamburg: "To erect in this state, opposite Augusta, a rival place of trade; to arrest an expected $2,000,000 worth of trade annually and hinder it from passing into Georgia; and to throw a large portion of that trade into your own port of Charleston."

Now, fifteen years later, amid controversy and in hopes of reassuring them that their confidence in him was not misplaced, he described the town as "a busy and thriving mart, rising into an opulent and populous town, its rapid achievement only due to unbounded command which I, an individual in every way humble, have been successful."

Next came a colorful list of what he endured in the process: "hostile interests, vexations of law, prison, terror, and the very pangs of death itself." After a few specifics about his treatment from "that other state," he softened his tone, lowered the bravado, and acknowledged that "Hamburg could not have succeeded if nature had not fitted the place for such an undertaking, Providence had not

74

smiled on it, or I, its instrument, had not found assistance of the State and the protecting arm of the Legislature. Upon my labors, fortune has smiled." Should they have forgotten, he reminded them what those major labors had been and how his ideas, at first, had been received.

In 1813, when I spoke of building a bridge, I was treated as wild and visionary. They told me that Wade Hampton, a great man of vast wealth and highest energy, had tried twice to accomplish such an enterprise, but the ruins are yet there to bear witness of his defeat. And now, they said, "Here we have a poor Dutchman, a poltroon of a pole boat on the Savannah River who talks about building a bridge." But the humble Dutchman, the despised boatman, calmly pursued the bold purpose, and bridled the rebellious stream which others had striven in vain to tame.

In 1816, I formed another design, and set to work. That was to build a wharf on the river at Augusta. Again the crowd jeered. "A wharf? People only build them at the seaside, where the tide only rises five to six feet. But on a stream that swells 20–30 feet? This man's mind is certainly unsound.

After that clamor, my next great plan was to build a town in the middle of a swamp. I was confident of restoring to South Carolina a trade on which Augusta had fattened for many years, and I promised to render to Charleston a large part of the commerce of Savannah and Augusta. The common opinion was that the strait jacket was necessary for me.

But my bridge has for 23 years withstood the fury of the mighty stream, with safe and easy passage. My wharf, after 20 years, is still unhurt from subsiding floods. And my town was not only built, but it wrested from Augusta that South Carolina trade which had belonged to her, and even fresh portions from Georgia.

My wharf obtained praise even from Europe. One princely traveler called it, 'The greatest and most useful structure he had ever seen.' Plus, three others have been erected nearby, and all are in successful operation.

Of my entire success, the founding of Hamburg and the benefits for the State I promised, I desire no higher testimony than that of 1833, when the Legislature relinquished the State's right and interest in the town to me.

That was also the year the legislature forgave the unpaid balance on his $50,000 loan.

Though the previous paragraph and compliment to the august body may sound like the perfect ending for his speech, Henry Shultz had more to say. Referring again to the loan, he told them how he used $15,000 to purchase his first steamboat and, right away, to begin direct steam navigation between Hamburg and Charleston. Then, as trade increased, that one boat led to purchasing six more. "Yes," he admitted, "when the railroad began their transport business there was alarm and some abandoning of the boat business. But experience shows passengers may prefer the railroad, while merchandise prefers the river." The steamboat business, he assured them, "is returning two for one."

His next topic concerned Hamburg's banks, starting with an explanation for why the first one, established in 1824, had failed: "The town was too new to have accumulated capital for investment. Without start-up funds, and for want of confidence from abroad, that bank was denied credit. But the fresh charter for another bank came with a specie capital of $500,000, of which $300,000 in gold and silver remains in the vaults, and renders the bank now in operation most successful."

Thus far, Shultz had carefully choreographed his presentation with a mixture of praise for himself, appreciation to the legislature for their help, and slight but entertaining reference to the negative treatment he incurred from his detractors. But scarcely a word after mentioning the Hamburg banks, his affable vocabulary dramatically changed.

Bank? Oh, here it comes. What he had written so far was but prologue. Now surfaced the primary reason for his memorial, beginning with a lashing tirade against his former nemesis, the Bank of the State of Georgia.

> But the Augusta bank suffers from grievous mischief of multiple paper banks, and pernicious methods, (and) I have been compelled to wage a continual war, not only with this wealthier and old rival of Hamburg, or also of Savannah, but the entire State of Georgia.
>
> Everything, all parts of the Government and the State have been employed to crush me and strangle my enterprise in its cradle. When imprisonments tried and failed, they resorted to allurements. When that failed, they turned to violence. Then came the great, general consolation of persecuting me by robbing me of the bridge I had built, trying to swindle you for granting me the charter, and levying tolls in a manner to encourage passage of produce to their town and to discourage it from their side to your town, all with tolls exorbitant and levied to favor their trade at your expense and that of Hamburg.

Then, in contrast to his own work, he followed with a long list of inferior or unfinished projects by others, including roads and turnpikes, railroad extensions, and even a $2,000,000 project by the

State of South Carolina for internal improvements, most of which was spent on canals now dried up and rivers now rendered less navigable than before.

> Let these undertakings be compared to any excellence of design, or to bare success with those set foot by me. Not one (of theirs) was carried to execution or accomplished its objects to the full.

After another summary of his superior works, he launched into a list of platitudes to explain why he had been so successful where others had not.

> My life, the purpose it pursued, what governed it, perhaps is not a little peculiar. Untaught, except in the School of Necessity, I have little beyond the Book of which nature, its truest teacher, holds up to those whom all other instructors pass disdainfully by. Unskilled in the artificial rules of Society, I am unversed in conventional sentiments, and far better acquainted with actions and their effects than with refinement of language.

> I have consulted Nature and her laws first, man and his laws second. I have held my counsel, made my prayer to Him only who rules Heaven and Earth. I ask for myself nothing from men. To be useful has always seemed to me the utmost attainment of excellence and happiness. Apart from this, gold I have never regarded but as trash. I've never asked for it, except to give wider effect to my usefulness. My labors were always more for the benefit of others than for myself. The very law that places man above creation is this: that he is capable of making his happiness by procuring that of others.

> I have made the plain dictates of the heart my guide, my main instrument, the natural gift of unshrinking resolution and perseverance. With these sentiments I have,

at last, after 15 years of difficulty and toil, lived to see all
my undertakings crowned with full success.

Finally, he really was drawing to a close, but not without another change in tone, a parting hint of apology, and one more topic to discuss. He hoped, "my recital (has achieved) the natural desire to appear not unworthy of esteem by this honorable body, but this was not my whole motive." That would be to address his newest project, something that had been in discussion for some time: starting direct trade between South Carolina and his native country, Germany.

It is my desire that my experience may be useful both
to the country of my birth, and that of my adoption, to
enlarge commerce between them. I am anxious, for this
purpose, to tender my voluntary services in any capacity
which seems good to you, and offered with sincere respect
and affection without the slightest idea of remuneration
or fee.

Following a few suggestions on how this transaction could be accomplished, he closed his narration with this farewell:

And now, I beg leave to tender to your honorable body
my very hearty thanks for the high honor, trust, and
confidence, which it has been your pleasure, at various
times, to repose in me.

I am, with the highest respect,

Henry Shultz,

Founder and Proprietor of Hamburg

December the 17th, 1836

CHAPTER 24

Swimming in a Sea of Praise

What a response! From legislators to the governor of South Carolina, and from business colleagues to journalists across the state, plaudits and praise poured in for Henry Shultz. "Henry," one might ask, "where are your critics?" They certainly were not evident in the sentiments below (Reminder: The following responses, along with his above-mentioned self-defense, may also be read in their entirety in the Arts & Heritage Center of North Augusta or in the Old Genealogy Society Library housed in the Tompkins Library in Edgefield, and in the nearby Old Genealogical Archives, in Edgefield.)

Governor George McDuffie wrote,

> In my opinion, Mr. Shultz is eminently distinguished for enterprise, sagacity, perseverance, and public spirit, of which his numerous monuments furnish ample testimony:
>
> ___His bridge across the Savannah River, is so constructed as to bid defiance to floods, an achievement often tried but never successful before, so greatly affecting two states.
>
> ___His wharf at Augusta, is highly useful, and the inland navigation between Hamburg and Charleston is a tribute to his sagacity.
>
> ___Finally, the Town of Hamburg, now standing upon solid foundation, a site he found a quagmire, now with 35,000–40,000 bales of cotton annually brought to market there. Now, a town standing at the head of the longest railroad in the world will be of great advantage for foreign

agents to purchase cotton directly from the market instead
of from speculators in New York, Philadelphia ... This
town, built by enterprise and indefatigable perseverance
of Henry Shultz, under fostering care and patronage of the
State of South Carolina ... now opens a new channel of
commerce, based upon principles of friendly reciprocity
which South Carolina has always cherished.

Several businessmen expressed hope that his new efforts for trade
on the other side of the Atlantic will be favorable, including this from
Mr. B. J. Earle:

This effort is worthy of your genius, enlightened by the
course of events which have characterized your other
undertakings, all which have contributed more to the
public good than your private fortunes. It affords me great
pleasure to bear testimony to your zeal and integrity, and
I express my hope that it will be successful for the town
and for Europe.

The following is from attorney Waddy Thompson Jr.:

I have been associated with you 15 years as your counsel,
also as law officer of the State of South Carolina.
Understanding your character, I have no hesitation in
saying, on the sagacity of future events or any undertaking,
you have an energy that no adverse circumstances can
subdue. I have not known your equal.

Similarly, Mr. William C. Preston stated,

Your past enterprises, despite difficulties requiring
uncommon genius to surmount, assure me that any project
conceived by you, prompted by your enlarged, benevolent
views, will be carried out with ability and ardor. I know
about your numerous embarrassments on the Savannah
frontier, and have admired your perseverance to overcome
them. I earnestly wish you success.

Charleston businessman J. Hamilton recalled his first meeting with Mr. Shultz, which took place during a visit to Charleston to seek support for establishing inland navigation to Hamburg:

> I was struck with the intelligence, clearness, and forecast
> of your views. Though many thought you visionary, I
> am happy that I sustained you, and we have both lived to
> see the splendid triumph of all you conceived and nobly
> executed. I consider you one of the finest men I know.

Railroad executive Jon T. Robertson offered a tangible tribute to the much admired Shultz:

> In thanks for his liberality and mark of respect, we tender
> to him free passage on the railroad, up and down, whenever
> it pleases him to visit Charleston.

Members of a legislative committee formed to study the idea of European trade also spoke highly of Shultz, which obviously influenced their opinion of the trade plan:

> I always have a positive reaction to whatever Henry Shultz
> proposes … He always promotes the interest of the State
> above himself.

> Having witnessed his unyielding spirit in the darkest
> hours of adversity … and having fought by his side as
> he warred manfully against states, towns, banks, judges,
> lawyers, and creditors innumerable, we are glad to witness
> his final triumphs.

> Henry has had his faults, as we all have, but his faults
> lean to virtue's side. He possesses less of selfishness than
> those of any other man living.

> He is the only man we ever saw, whom the public
> could not prevent from doing the public good.

Most of the newspaper articles, of which there were many, wrote mainly on that one topic—the prospect of trade with Europe. Almost without exception, reporters, too, were equally profuse in their praise of Henry Shultz.

A writer with the *Charleston Mercury* complimented

> our energetic fellow citizen, Mr. Shultz, for his efforts to establish direct trade between Hamburg in this state and the most important commercial points of the European Continent. Intelligence like this is like a ray from a morning star telling of the coming dawn.

The following also came from the *Mercury*:

> Mr. Shultz deserves gratitude for his public spirited energy ... hoping this is just one of a series of enterprises, all tending to advance southern prosperity, and give safety and stability to southern institutions.

The *South Carolinian* praised him for what he had overcome as well as for his brilliance:

> Readers can see in our paper today the ever active mind of Mr. Shultz, now engaged in a most important enterprise, direct trade with Europe. We can say that no man in this State has erected half as many monuments to his genius as Henry Shultz. It is also known that his path is not all strewn with roses. He has passed through a most fiery ordeal, yet he has surmounted difficulties which, to others, were insurmountable. When darkest gloom settled on his prospects, more than once we have seen him accomplish what appeared almost magical. Knowing his extraordinary talent ... we don't question any scheme he may suggest.

And from across the river, in an editorial called, "Mr. Shultz's New Enterprise," the *Augusta Chronicle* wrote,

> We hope that, in his expected, well deserved success, he will also consider shipping to his European friends from Savannah, a seaport in our State. Our Savannah friends

will do well to exert themselves on behalf of a preference
so important to the commercial interest of that city.

An olive leaf, perhaps? After all, it had been fifteen years since
Mr. Shultz left their state. And no matter how grudgingly, Augusta
had to have noticed the phenomenal rise of that once little town across
the river.

Let's pause now from the euphoria surrounding Henry Shultz
and check on the mood and conditions in that still growing town
of Hamburg.

CHAPTER 25

The Leading Interior Market of South Carolina

In addition to managing a well-stocked grocery store, Hamburg resident Samuel Bowers must have been just as busy wearing his other hat as owner of the S. E. Bowers Realty Co. It may be difficult to prove one reporter's estimate of nearly two hundred storekeepers and traders in Hamburg by the time of the town's leading interior market reputation in 1835, but there's no doubt the S. E. Bowers Realty Co. had its hands full negotiating property and building space for the bustling business district emerging in downtown Hamburg at the time.

Listing every known 1830–1850 Hamburg business establishment here would be difficult if not unwise. Missing or incorrect records could disappoint someone's descendants, and multiple pages of phone-book-style information would hardly be palatable reading for others. Still, a selection of those shops, services, and other community opportunities about which we do have credible records should give us an informative, interesting, and maybe surprising picture of that place and those times.

Knowing as we do of Henry Shultz's penchant for getting the word out, it's not surprising that one of Hamburg's earliest services was a printing office, or that the town's first newspaper, the *Hamburg Gazette,* rolled off their presses on a royal-sized sheet in 1822. Not much is known of the content or longevity of that first publication, but the Arts and Heritage Center of North Augusta still has images of the *Gazette* and a number of later Hamburg papers in their files, including the *Carolina Galaxy*, which appeared for the first time on October 4, 1834.[31] Owner William M. Pritchard outlined the lofty purpose of his publication with this editorial:

> Today we introduce to our readers the first number of our paper, and make our debut in the editorial world. The principles and character of this paper were briefly delineated in our prospectus some weeks ago, and we now enter upon the task of discharging those duties, with the hope, however extravagant it may be, of pleasing all, and of offending none, extending the warm hand of cordiality and friendship to everyone, and desirous of cooperating in every means that will result in the prosperity of our common country, and to the advancement of the social comfort, happiness, and moral refinement of our people.

Another paper, the *Republican*, with the motto, "Ask nothing but what is right, and submit to nothing that is wrong," printed information about what was new, available, or happening in their town. One such ad, with the distinct flavor of mid-nineteenth-century advertising, announced the opening of a new tin factory "opposite the Carolina Hotel and next door to Dr. Creighton's Drug Store, where every article of tin, copper and iron ware will be made and sold on more reasonable terms than they ever have been in this market … Every article needed by housekeepers will be made to order, and sold as low as they can be bought in Charleston … Call on us before purchasing elsewhere at old prices."

No matter how many "numbers" the *Galaxy* or the *Republican* printed, or years they remained in service, the Hamburg newspaper with a lengthy life span then and the most surviving references now seems to have been the *Hamburg Journal*. The *Journal* began publication on April 7, 1840, as a semiweekly paper and was "devoted to foreign and domestic news, markets, literature, and science." Editor John W. Yarborough had sky-high goals for his publication. Believing that the growing importance of Hamburg as a flourishing trade market needed "a vehicle of trade and intelligence," he promised to give "unbiased political news, with slander and abuse carefully excluded, and to offer market and trade news valuable to businesses from every part of the Union." The paper would be "of extraimperial size, with good type on white paper, and cost five dollars per annum, payable in advance." Perhaps they would reap the balance of needed profit and expense money from their long list of advertisers, including but not limited to the following:

- a livery stable at the rear of the Old American Hotel, opposite the railroad depot, where horses might be boarded for ten dollars a month or fifty cents a day, or receive a single feed for twenty-five cents
- Mrs. Smith's upholstering shop, which had beautiful bedding for sale and would also neatly repair any mattress made out of hair, cotton, or moss
- Dr. J. H. Murray, who offered his professional services to citizens of Hamburg from his office in Cooke's Drug Store (with Mr. Cooke also advertising his services)
- George Parrott, who sold nails of Swedish iron, sugar, and hemp bagging
- B. C. Yancey, attorney at law, who attended to professional business in the districts of Edgefield, Abbeville, Barnwell, and Augusta, Georgia.

But not even advertising income could keep Mr. Yarborough in business for long. It must have been a sad day when his company declared bankruptcy in 1842, just two years after the *Hamburg Journal* was born. Fortunately, lofty motives or not, the more successful partnership of Thomas G. Key and Henry D. Wray managed to rescue the paper and keep it in production at least past the 1850s.

Sandwiched between the aforementioned hotels, grocery and clothing stores, and items advertised above, Hamburg shoppers found plenty of other goods, imported or homemade, at their disposal too. This list included hardware cutlery, watches and jewelry, drapery and tailor-made clothing, and one historic Hamburg enterprise advertised as "Superior Eight-Day Brass Clocks, warranted to keep first-rate time," made and sold by L. M. Churchill & Co. Some of these clocks are found in local homes to this day or may be seen in the Hamburg exhibit at the Arts and Heritage Center of North Augusta.

Considering the large number of horses also housed in Hamburg, we must not forget the many shops that existed especially for them and for those who owned them. Besides the livery stable behind the American Hotel, two other stables, one operated by Charles Hammond and the other by A. W. Roach, offered similar services with competing prices. An assortment of finished leathers for harness making could be purchased at R. T. Henderson's Currying Shop, while carriage maker Patrick Curran might sell you a new carriage or repair the one you already had. Still other businesses sold shoes, boots, hats, saddles, and other accessories needed or desired by the horse-owning public.[32]

However, none of these later enterprises replaced the original purpose of the town. Two steamboat companies still sold, serviced, and operated the boats that, along with the added services of the railroad, transported trade to and from Hamburg and the port cities of Charleston and Savannah. Nor had the town's warehouses ever been busier, as more and more cotton, tobacco, and other farm produce remained in those spacious storage facilities between their arrival in Hamburg and their purchase or shipment to their final destinations. Trading companies, such as cotton merchants Hammond & Lark, also conducted business in the waterfront area.

CHAPTER 26

Hamburg: A Nice Place for Men and Ladies to Live

Hamburg was more than "the leading interior market of South Carolina." (See previous chapter). It was a community, a place where people with common interests and abilities could meet to learn, serve, or share time and activities with each other. We already know about the Hamburg Mechanic's Society, whose members included builders, craftsmen, and men in similar laboring professions. We also know of L. B. Holloway's Billiard Room, where those laborers might have gone to unwind after a hard day's work. Men could also join the Harmony Lodge of Free and Accepted Masons.

And what about the women? While men were out enjoying themselves, was there nothing for them to do but stay home, keep house, and tend children? Not at all. At some point, a new organization emerged especially for them. Though called simply "the Ladies of Hamburg," what happened at their meetings was neither simple nor ordinary. This was more than a social group for escaping the toils of their day; these ladies met to serve. By the early 1850s, because of a project sparked by one particular South Carolina woman, the Ladies of Hamburg would receive national recognition for this and other service-related activities.

She was not from Hamburg herself, but Ann Pamela Cunningham, raised not far away on the prosperous Rosemont Plantation near Greenwood, South Carolina, had an idea she could not accomplish alone. Sadly, while still in her teens, Ann Pamela suffered a severe spinal injury after falling from a horse. Though her parents took her to Philadelphia for long-term treatment, she remained partially paralyzed for the rest of her life.

One day in 1853, as her mother, Louisa Byrd Cunningham, was returning home by steamboat after visiting Ann Pamela in Philadelphia, she noticed the badly deteriorating condition of Mount Vernon, the former home of President George Washington, who had died some fifty years before. Chagrined by the sight of this national landmark along the banks of the Potomac River, Louisa Byrd described the building's neglected condition in a letter to her daughter. Ann Pamela might have been hampered in body, but nothing was wrong with her spirit. There was still something she could do with her life.

Her first action was to write a letter, via the *Charleston Mercury* and other southern newspapers, to "The Ladies of the South," asking them to begin raising funds to purchase and renovate Mount Vernon. The Ladies of Hamburg were among the first to respond.

The next year, after various women's groups had banded together to become the Mount Vernon Ladies' Association, the Hamburg ladies elected officers, determined rules and duties, and proposed the name "Hamburg Mount Vernon Association" as appropriate for their branch of the larger organization. According to the *Augusta Chronicle* of April 15, 1854, "the name was hailed with enthusiasm and greeted with unanimous approval." Also, the *Chronicle* continued, "Quite a handsome sum was raised, and from this happy beginning, the most cheering results are promised." Included in this "handsome sum" was a $550 donation from Mr. William Gregg, founder of the nearby Graniteville Company cotton mill.

The Mount Vernon mansion, located on Washington's family-owned land, was built by George's elder brother Lawrence in 1743.

The future president acquired the property in stages over the next two decades, made multiple improvements to house and landscape, and lived there when not at war or in the presidency until his death in 1799. A succession of Washington descendants fell heir to the property until, by the time Miss Cunningham and her organization began their attempts to purchase and restore it, Mount Vernon was owned by the president's great-grandnephew John Augustine Washington. Although John Augustine had fallen on hard times and was unable to make necessary repairs to the property, he resisted efforts to part with his beloved family heritage.

But Ann Pamela was persistent too. In 1856, prior to her dealings with the owner, she applied to the State of Virginia for a Mount Vernon Ladies' Association charter. The legislature granted her request and acknowledged her as the organization's first regent. Rumor has it that after repeated requests to make the purchase failed, she had a talk with Mr. Washington's wife. It took more time, but in 1860, after the Mount Vernon ladies had raised the agreed-upon price of $200,000, Washington finally agreed to sell the property to them.

Ann Pamela Cunningham died in 1875, but the association she founded is considered one of the most successful historic preservation programs in the country. To date, no taxpayer money has been used to support this national treasure. Through gift and souvenir sales on the premises, private donations, and entrance fees from approximately one million visitors a year, the still surviving Mount Vernon Ladies' Association continues to own, maintain, and revere the home of America's first president, George Washington.

In a final but important note on this subject, even though Miss Cunningham made her first request for such an organization to "the Ladies of the South," the word "South" never appears in any of the association's names. Right from the start, as noted in that 1854

Augusta Chronicle article summarizing the Hamburg ladies' branch of the organization, the local chapter agreed with one of the major resolutions of the Mount Vernon project: "As (President) Washington belonged to no particular section or people, but to the whole American republic, we recommend to all true-hearted Americans who are the recipients of his glorious legacy, this stirring appeal." Thus, though still primarily a women's organization, from that day to this, the appeal spread and continues to receive response from all across America.

The Mount Vernon project may have been the first effort by the Ladies of Hamburg to reach outside their town, but it would not be their last. It was now 1861, the nation was at war, and they had work that only Southern women could do. This time, as compiled in a March 18, 1863, report in the *Augusta Chronicle*, their hearts and hands were geared toward "bettering the lives of the Confederate soldiers." The article continues with this heartfelt response from one of those soldiers: "Capt. Croft of the 22nd South Carolina returned thanks to the Hamburg women for their generous efforts in sending 240 useful articles and garments to the hospital at Ringgold, Georgia, 167 garments to the 7th South Carolina Regiment the December before, and for making 569 articles of clothing, blankets, etc., since November of the previous year."

As if saving the best for last, the article concludes with this final comment: "The Hamburg Ladies have made uniforms for six Confederate Companies since the war began." Not a bad résumé for a small group of women from that once little town of Hamburg, South Carolina.[33]

How nice it would be to conclude our story here with "and they lived happily ever after." But Hamburg was a real place where real people lived, had downturns as well as successes, and experienced sorrows amid their joys. To tell that other side, we need to turn back a few years, recap some prior events, and learn what else happened in the life of Henry Shultz after we left him at the center of attention with the state legislature in 1836, as well as what happened to the town some have lovingly called "his offspring."

CHAPTER 27

Sometimes Plans Go Awry

For all his accomplishments and well-deserved accolades, Henry Shultz also left a trail of unfinished business in his wake. Some of his grandest ideas, even when at first well-received, never reached their intended outcome.

We could begin while he was still in Germany, known by his birth name of Klaus Hinrich Klahn, and appearing to operate a highly successful shipping business. (See chapter 2). But when war complicated his own indebtedness, he literally jumped ship, changed his name, and came to America to start over. Success seemed within his grasp again in Brunswick, Georgia, where he acquired a pole-boat business and proposed building a canal between the Altamaha River and nearby tidal rivers to improve water accessibility in and around southeast Georgia towns, but this project was never approved by the state.

Once again, because the Savannah River does not flow all the way to Charleston, Schultz realized how much easier it would be for his newly acquired steamboats to travel between the river and Charleston if the narrow and shallow portions of that passageway were made deeper and wider. Yet, we search the record today for news about the project and find little except an occasional sentence saying the project was never completed. Eventually we do learn "the planned waterway project near Charleston could not be completed because of a prior agreement between Georgia and South Carolina regarding navigation and shared use of the Savannah River."[34]

So will the much-heralded trade between the lands of his birth and adoption be the proverbial third time that never fails for Henry Shultz?

When mentioning his international trade plan to the legislature in 1836, Shultz was not suggesting the idea; he was campaigning for it. The movement was well underway by then, and they knew it. More than a year before, he and others had organized, and the legislature had chartered, their American and German Trading and Insurance Company. Half the shares of company stock, worth $1,000 each, were to be sold in Germany, and the other half in the United States. Stock sales, however, were slow to support the enthusiasm of the organizers. But that may not have been their only problem.

As with those earlier plans along the Georgia and South Carolina coasts, there were unknown laws or conditions concerning international trade as well. That explains why, after about five years of negotiation, when organizers determined that those existing international trade laws would complicate, or even prevent, their much desired Hamburg-to-Hamburg trade, both the company and its trading plan ceased to exist. Bureaucracy, it seems, along with insufficient knowledge and preparation, foiled an otherwise popular and well-intentioned idea.

There's still more to tell about both the founder and residents of Hamburg as the 1830s turned into the 1840s and beyond. At the same time, other events beyond their control would intervene and cause more of their plans to go awry.

CHAPTER 28

Did All Roads Still Lead to Hamburg?

They rose fast, Shultz and his town. By 1823, just two years after the settlement began, Hamburg had become a well-populated, fully functioning trading center, and the momentum would not stop for at least two decades. But when it did, the reversal was rapid too. In contrast, although what happened in the town affected the life of the founder and vice versa, the saga of Henry Shultz could be titled "More of the Same."

If we've learned anything about Henry Shultz so far, it's that his life more closely resembled a roller-coaster ride than a steady uphill climb. He might achieve a major accomplishment, follow with a period of financial distress, and then, against all odds, bounce back again. Likewise, he could be hailed for his genius one moment and face an angry creditor or associate the next. Even the State of South Carolina alternated between heaping him with praise, threatening to confiscate his town when he didn't honor his side of their agreements, and then forgiving a large part of those very obligations. When Shultz overcame his difficulties with the state, however, we know the reason why. They needed him to keep the cotton flowing to Charleston more than he needed them. With or without the state, this up-and-down movement continued to the end of his life. Bankruptcies? There were several, including the initial one in 1827, resulting in imprisonment and the sale of some of his property; another in 1834, with more property sales; and finally, in 1842, a greater diminishing of his assets, from which he never fully recovered. But before then, following his highly positive interaction with the legislature in 1836, and about the time the international trade idea came to an end, he had an experience some have called the crest of his success.

The year 1840, besides seeing the loss of anticipated revenue from international trade, was the year the City of Augusta purchased the bridge from its private owner and made it permanently toll-free for all cotton or produce wagons crossing into or out of Augusta. The result was obvious and intentional. Traders now had the option of going on to that larger trading center across the river instead of stopping in Hamburg. The town, the state, and especially the port city of Charleston were alarmed.

True to form, Shultz once again had an idea. He would go to Charleston and talk with other concerned citizens about ways to counteract Augusta's bid for the now presumed South Carolina trade. His suggestions included asking the South Carolina Railroad Company to build additional warehouses for storing cotton in Hamburg, urging agencies of the state bank with sufficient funds to both purchase cotton and advance loans on stored cotton, and, finally, requesting that a line of boats be available on the Savannah River for exclusive employment in the transportation of produce to Charleston.[35]

As usual, his fellow tradesmen were more than impressed. Right away an advisory committee recommended that all three suggestions be adopted.

If anything, Charleston's response to his plan was mild compared to the reception awaiting him in Hamburg. Calling his expedition "a successful trade mission," the *Edgefield Advertiser* described the scene like this: "All the houses in Hamburg were illuminated, his arrival by boat was announced by an artillery salute, and he was escorted through the streets in a coach drawn by four white horses.

A brass band led the parade, after which a sumptuous collation was served on Shultz Hill."[36]

So how soon did the Charleston and Hamburg partnership begin to implement these grand plans? The answer may be in the word "crest," which refers to the height of something, not necessarily an indication of things to come. Thus, as Rosser Taylor explains, "The reception of Mr. Shultz at the hands of his fellow-townsmen in honor of his successful trade mission proved to be premature, for Charleston was then vastly more interested in the Charleston and Cincinnati railway project and, consequently, gave little or no support to the recommendations of the committee."[37]

Railway? Ah, yes. Seven years had passed since the Charleston and Hamburg Railroad Company began its historic train service between the two locations—seven years for the railroad concept to spread, other companies to form, and new rail lines to extend in many directions. The C&HRR itself merged or expanded into new companies and continued to operate under a variety of names. On December 19, 1843, and for the next four decades, that name became, simply, "the South Carolina Railroad."

Although the Charleston and Cincinnati Railroad never materialized, in time other extensions would successfully connect from the original C&HRR tracks to other parts of the state—often nearer where the farmers lived, relieving them of the need to deliver their produce to the trading center themselves. Now, too, some of the new lines connected directly to Columbia or ran all the way to Charleston, bypassing Hamburg altogether.

But not yet. Nor were the railroads the only reason the once vibrant town of Hamburg would soon become a way station instead of a destination. The tide was about to turn again, as Augusta found additional ways to regain the lost trade that once belonged to them.

CHAPTER 29

Back to the River

The railroad may have brought new vitality to the trade, transportation, and total economy of the two-state area, but the Savannah River, that primary magnet for attracting early settlers to the American Southeast, retained its role as the most important resource, natural or otherwise, for the people of Georgia and South Carolina.

Yes, the river could be a problem, especially when rainfall extremes caused flooding or drought, or where obstacles and shallow water made navigation hazardous or impossible. However, although floods, some with disastrous effects, would recur well into the next century, or until completion of the Clarks Hill (now Thurmond) Dam in 1956, people learned to live with the river, or at least diminish its dangers.

They deepened the channels near the shore to improve docking and navigation, placed homes and businesses farther from the water to minimize flooding, and, thanks to Lewis Cooper, Henry Shultz, and others, built bridges strong enough to withstand the brunt of the river's power. But, as Augusta knew all too well, one river hazard continued to make navigation all the way into the city impossible. That would be the so-called Savannah Rapids—not the late-twentieth-century community building in Columbia County, but the too swift, too shallow stretch of water nearby, for which the building is named.

Unlike upstate or inland South Carolina farmers, upstate Georgia farmers living near the river could still bring their produce most of the way to Augusta by boat rather than travel through the forest along crude or barely existent roadways. But when reaching that hazardous section of the river, their best route was to unload their boats on the South Carolina side, transfer to wagons, and deliver their goods to Hamburg. Of course, that often meant eventual delivery to Charleston, not Savannah—trade advantage South Carolina, not Georgia—at least until bridge tolls were removed in 1840. Even then, the route was still longer and more time-consuming.

But Augusta had more problems than just lost trade, for which two somewhat simultaneous events could be blamed. Soil depletion and falling markets near the end of the 1830s caused a decline in cotton production, while continued settlement of America's western lands lured a number of her residents to "go west"—to Alabama, Mississippi, and even Texas—in search of new land or opportunity. Augusta definitely needed something to strengthen the local economy, and prominent attorney Henry Cumming thought he knew just what that something might be.

Because of soil composition, canals may not have been feasible statewide. But along Georgia's fall line, where the rocky piedmont joins the softer bedrock of the upper coastal plain, Cumming not only believed a canal extending from the river was possible but also felt that such a channel would provide enough water power to attract much-needed replacement industry to the area. Based on his study of older European canals and inspection of the ones newly built or under construction in this country, Cumming had a good understanding of the subject. He also knew where to turn for advice about building a similar waterway nearer home.

John Edgar Thomson, chief engineer for the nearly completed Georgia Railroad, was about to return to his native Pennsylvania when Cumming approached him for advice and for help in planning the proposed canal. That's why, in November 1844, instead of packing for Pennsylvania, Thomson was on a mission with Cumming and a handful of other community leaders to determine whether a canal could be built along the river and, if so, whether the midriver channel Bull Sluice, just over the Columbia County line, was the best place to begin. Yes was the answer to all the above, including Thomson's two-year extension in Augusta to survey the land and map the canal's route.

Work on the canal began in the spring of 1845, barely six months after the Cumming-Thomson party took their exploratory hike from Augusta to Bull Sluice. Eighteen months later, on November 23, 1846, an also newly-built diversion dam began redirecting water from the river into the canal from the head gates to the end of level one at Augusta's Thirteenth Street basin, seven miles away. By 1848, another two levels would be added, making the completed canal nine miles long.

Because they built it, did industry come? Did it ever! Thanks to a fifty-two-foot drop in elevation from the headgates to the city of Augusta, the downward flow through the canal provided exactly the water power Henry Cumming had envisioned. Within a few years, at least seventy factories, mills, and related businesses were benefiting from that power and providing jobs and commerce to benefit the local economy besides—all this and something else no one saw coming at the time.

A little more than a decade after completion of the canal, when war clouds loomed over the nation again, the newly declared Confederate States of America president, Jefferson Davis, chose the Augusta Canal as the site for the only powder works complex ever built to supply munitions for the Confederate Army. Spacious river banks, allowing enough room for twenty-six buildings along a two-mile stretch on both sides of the canal, plus the abundance of water power for turning factory turbines, had clinched the decision to locate such a vital facility along the Augusta Canal.[38]

But weren't we talking about the trade war between Georgia and South Carolina, not the one-sided Augusta economy, as the reason to include the Augusta Canal as part of our story? As we know, rancor, anger, or, as some have suggested, "Augusta's revenge" for Hamburg's taking of her long established trade has been a good part of our theme ever since Henry Shultz crossed the river with revenge on *his* mind for the taking of his bridge. Herein lies an interesting twist to that rivalry.

Yes, Augusta or the Augusta Bank took the bridge, made it toll-free for their side of the river, and resisted the Hamburg effort from the start. Then, when roles changed and Hamburg appeared to be winning that trade war at Augusta's expense, each side had work to do: Hamburg to keep the trade on their side, Augusta to get it back.

The purpose of the canal really was to aid the city. That it also completely restored Georgia's upriver trade to her side of the river was a by-product, another benefit for their side, if you will, and perhaps a chance to gloat that the Augusta Canal had placed another nail in Hamburg's coffin.

From wherever they came, other "nails" also had names. About 1848 one of these was the Greenville and Columbia Railway, which was bringing rail service into western South Carolina for the first time. Soon afterward, the South Carolina Railroad itself added a similar branch to Camden to benefit the central part of the state.

But the largest nail of all took place in 1853 when the same South Carolina Railroad, whose original owners had established that first rail service between Charleston and Hamburg, built a bridge across the river into Augusta, thereby connecting to the Georgia Railroad, to all points south toward Savannah, and to a growing number of destinations in the western part of the state and beyond.

Hamburg was not a stop on any of those new lines.

CHAPTER 30

The Death of Henry Shultz and the Near Death of His Town

They rose together, Shultz and his town, their lifespans similar in length but overlapping. He was forty-five when he birthed the town, where he lived and worked for thirty years before his death. Hamburg lingered on through a variety of stages until she became scarcely a shadow of her early days by the end of the century.

Obviously, when cotton production slowed, the European trade venture fell apart, and railroad extensions, plus the Augusta Canal, all but destroyed the reason for Hamburg's existence, the days of high achievement for Henry Shultz were also over. Without trade or traders, his boats remained docked, the warehouses stood empty, and most of his business operations declined or ceased operation altogether. With all these obstacles, plus his record of financial overextension, it's no wonder his bankruptcy in 1842 brought an end to both his enterprising life and, sadder still, even his ability to provide for his own needs. Once again his properties were assigned to trustees, who parceled them out to pay off his debts. After this, whether fortunately or ashamedly, he was left with little alternative except to live off the charity of his friends.

Apart from a few scant reports, details about the personal side of Henry Shultz have always left us with more questions than answers. Surprisingly, for a man who was so public, even boastful, about his business life, we rarely hear him say anything about his private life. But there may be a reason for the latter. This was the nineteenth century, and if the following records are accurate, any man, especially an immigrant living in the American South, may not have thought it wise to relinquish that privacy.

The earliest mention we have of a Shultz family is the brief March 30, 1827, announcement in a New York newspaper that "Henry Shultz, of Hamburg, married Miss Fanny Edee, of that city." Though the bride was from New York, we don't know in what city or state the wedding took place. And we have no knowledge of a Mrs. Shultz joining in the Mechanic's Society festivities later that year in Hamburg or visiting her new husband in jail after his part in the death of a suspected thief. (See chapters 14–15.)

Were there children? Apparently so, though we wouldn't have this evidence for at least a dozen more years, and only then from Edgefield District census reports. The first, in 1840, lists one Henry Shultz as having "a spouse and five black children." Their names and ages are not given, and there are other reports that some of the children, instead of belonging to the couple, may have been freed Black slaves. By the 1850 census, the Shultz entry had dwindled to "Henry, 74 years of age, and one black female, Meriah, 30 years old," who could have been his daughter, reports say[39] Thus, we may have part of the mystery solved, such as why the census-taker seems to be the only person who reveals both who, and of what race, the occupants of the Shultz household were. But we are left to guess much more, such as what happened to all the others, and why, except for Meriah, his only latter-year companions seem to have been his charitable friends. His mixed-race family, however, may explain, whether disclosed or not, why he was known to be friendly to slaves.

So ends even a scarcity of news about the once prolific, energetic Henry Shultz. So too, on October 5, 1851, ends his life. The *Edgefield Advertiser* noted his passing with this obituary:

> We have to announce the death of Henry Shultz, the
> founder of the town of Hamburg in this district. He expired
> at his residence on Monday night last. Mr. Shultz was a
> remarkable man and his energies were called out through
> a large portion of a long life in works of great usefulness
> to the community in which he lived ... There were few
> men of his day and time who possessed more of the high
> spirit of disinterested enterprise. He contended against
> adversity with the fortitude of a true hero. He smiled amid
> reverses of fortune, many of which befell him, and sank
> into his final rest undaunted to the last. His name cannot
> readily be forgotten by the community with which he was
> identified.[40]

No, the name of Henry Shultz has not been forgotten, even
if exactly where he is buried, other than in an unmarked grave
somewhere on Shultz Hill, is another mystery we still have about
him. But a couple of traditions concerning his burial have survived:
first, that he asked to be buried standing up, facing Augusta, so he
could keep an eye on her activities; or, second, that he be sitting up
with his back to Augusta, representing the anger he never resolved
against the city that did him wrong.[41]

The timing of his death, however, was a paradox. Mercifully,
his town, although in decline for reasons already mentioned, was
still alive as a community when he died, and Henry Shultz never
witnessed the death of his beloved offspring.

On the other hand, perhaps akin to the proverbial agony and
ecstasy, two of those charitable friends, James Jones and Joseph
Kennedy, were doing much more than caring for his physical needs
during the final years of his life. While serving as his end-of-life
administrators, they also had taken on his lifelong cause, believing as
he did that the bridge all those years ago really should have reverted

to him. In early 1855, three and a half years after his death, the courts agreed. The long-lingering case *Henry Shultz vs. The Bank of the State of Georgia* was settled in Shultz's favor. Jones and Kennedy accepted the $7,500 award on their friend's behalf.[42]

It was said of Henry Shultz that he died as he arrived in this country, "empty pockets upon arrival, penniless at the end of his life." But, remembering his own stated view of money as "trash" during his 1836 memorial (see chapter 23), or as something he used only to make his benevolences more successful, had he known about the final disposition of his bridge case, he would have claimed victory in the greatest battle of his life after all—not for the money, perhaps, but for the recovery of his "good name."

Just as Henry Shultz could not continue his high-achievement life without the prosperity of his town, neither could the people continue to exist without the trade and traffic for which their town was created. The traders themselves may have had the most to lose when, for economic survival, their companies moved elsewhere. But when most of those wagonloads of people, tent cities, and sporadic shoppers no longer had reason to come to Hamburg, the town's merchants were victims too. Furthermore, as an outgrowth from the loss of business and trade, both the local bank and its currency became worthless by the time of the Civil War, reducing the likelihood of new enterprise moving into Hamburg.

Gradually, the majority of residents also moved away. Some stayed past the beginning of the war, including the busy Ladies of Hamburg and those with employment or other connections in nearby Augusta who chose to remain in their homes. Still, by war's end, only a scattered few claimed Hamburg as their address.

But not long afterward, following what have been called Hamburg's forgotten years, a dramatic change took place in the former trading center. After considering how the war also changed cities and towns in South Carolina and all across the South, we'll learn how, according to another Hamburg tradition, the town without a people became home for a people without a town.

CHAPTER 31

The Daunting Aftermath of War

Mathematics, physics, and astronomy are among the branches of knowledge we call exact sciences. History, that infinite conglomeration of the past, is not on the list. Yes, from personal data to national and international events, from the most celebrated occurrences to the smallest detail of what happened when, where, and to whom, many facts can be verified without dispute. But sometimes, as within well-rehearsed family or community lore, phrases like "That's not the way I heard it" compete strongly with what others consider settled fact.

Take Hamburg, South Carolina, for example. If you had inquired about the emerging town across the river from Augusta in the early to mid-1800s, you might have heard, "Oh, isn't that the town where Henry Shultz put up the fronts of a half dozen buildings in just one night and had one hundred houses full of people in only two months' time?" (See chapter 9.) As we now know, yes, the town grew fast, but not quite at that speed. And today, despite many years of celebrated achievement, most people have little knowledge about the former town except "Oh, isn't that where they had a big riot and a lot of people got killed?"

Along with time lapse and faulty memories, South Carolina historian, Dr. Walter Edgar adds, "We don't judge history by the culture of today." For this reason, we need to review now what we do know was happening across the South in the years between the war and this point in our story. Specifically, the four years of the Civil

War may have been over by April 1865, but disruption in the lives of everyone who survived and remained would last much longer.

On January 1, 1863, or about midway through the conflict, President Lincoln issued his Emancipation Proclamation, freeing slaves in all but a few counties in the eleven Confederate States. Two years later, Congress passed the Thirteenth Amendment, which by war's end would permanently outlaw slavery anywhere in the country. By December 1865, this amendment was ratified by the required three-fourths of states that remained in the Union, plus all states readmitted following dissolution of the Confederacy.[43] Within five years, two more amendments to the Constitution were added: the fourteenth, granting citizenship to all persons born or naturalized in the United States, and the fifteenth, which declared, "the right of citizens of the United States to vote shall not be denied ... on account of race, color, or previous condition of servitude." Together, these three amendments were known as "The Negro's Bill of Rights."[44]

But what those amendments may have done for the former slaves, now called freedmen, was not necessarily good for the plantation owners. In addition to ruined or confiscated land, they now faced the problem of diminished or more expensive labor. Not to minimize the celebrated end of slavery, but the loss of that partnership between master/owner and slave labor also meant a new way of life for the freedmen. With freedom came increased personal responsibility. So many questions—What would they do now? Where would they live? How would their needs be met?—were new to them. All these decisions, formerly made for them or, conversely, assuring them of their daily provision, they now had to make for themselves.

Recognizing this need, to cite a common phrase, the US government "came to help." In 1867, that help was called Reconstruction, and it consisted of the Freedmen's Bureau, a program to aid the former slaves in their move from forced labor to independence, plus units of federal troops to quell any difficulty or disturbance this shift in nearly two centuries of accustomed interdependence might cause.

Sounds like a good plan. Did it work? Perhaps in theory, but history—the factual kind—says otherwise, and for understandable reasons. Mainly, three groups of people were attempting to do something few, if any, of them had ever done before. Not only were adjustments required for the plantation owners and former slaves, but those who managed the Freedmen's Bureau were also breaking new ground. Besides coming primarily from the still unforgiven North—a glaring stumbling block in the first place—those who came to help had been asked to create the country's first-ever government welfare plan. Because of so many unknowns, few people at the time, or when assessing the bureau to this day, would disagree with the word "stumbling" being used to define how well or how effective their work turned out to be.

Along with lingering White resistance to those three Negro rights amendments, the bureau also underestimated the sheer size of the Black population. Even before the war, the number of slaves in several southern states exceeded the number of Whites. This was especially true in South Carolina, where, according to the 1860 census, of the state's more than 703,000 residents, at least 402,000 were Black slaves. Now, following the war and emancipation, former slaves swarming into the area essentially doubled the size of nearby Augusta, compounding the resettling problem in that city as well as other urban centers by creating four times as many freedmen seeking employment as there were jobs for them to do.[45]

Despite all these obstacles, Reconstruction did accomplish or make a good start toward a number of later successes. In something of a building boom, new schools provided education to formerly untaught Black children, while new hospitals, orphanages, and other public services offered a variety of care and assistance to Blacks as well as Whites. Also, as author Eric Foner writes in his appropriately titled book *Reconstruction*, within a few years, "the small but growing number of black landowners, businessmen, and professionals opened a door that did not close ... and never would they return to closely supervised gang labor."[46]

But, from whatever point of view, this experiment in our country's past is filled with far more reports of failure than success. In Foner's opinion, "Reconstruction was the most controversial and misunderstood period in all of American history."[47]

In 1876, the year of our nation's first centennial, something happened in Hamburg, South Carolina, that, in just one more year, would contribute greatly to Reconstruction's demise.

CHAPTER 32

A Place of Their Own

The once prosperous trading center might never again be called the leading interior market of South Carolina (see chapter 25), but for a few years following the war, the little town served a necessary and very practical purpose. Some of those empty homes and business facilities were about to be filled again. By the late 1860s, Hamburg had become "a place of their own" for several hundred newly displaced freedmen.

But lest we think the Freedmen's Bureau just dropped them off and settled them on available land to fend for themselves, we know from the record that capable, educated, and otherwise accomplished persons were among those new Hamburg residents. How could this be?

Not all slaves were forced to, or even chose to, wait for emancipation before they were freed. In addition to more than a few escapees, from the time of the American Revolution—and perhaps by taking to heart the line from the Declaration of Independence that "all men are created equal (and) endowed by their Creator with certain unalienable rights"—some slave owners, first in the North and later in the South, began freeing slaves of their own accord. By the time of the Civil War, an estimated 250,000 free Blacks were already living in the South.[48] That number rose substantially during Reconstruction when former southern Blacks living in the North returned home, presumably to fulfill another of the bureau's initiatives to reconnect the freedmen with family members who already were free.

For the most part, through education, opportunity, and personal motivation, those earlier free Blacks had a head start on their newly freed counterparts. Thus, much like a parent or teacher, they served as leaders and role models, first in their families, and then in their communities and beyond. The fascinating story of one such former slave helps set the stage for what is about to happen in the newly resettled town of Hamburg.

He was born into slavery in Beaufort County, South Carolina; became a favored house slave on a wealthy rice plantation; and, against normal slave protocol at the time, was taught to read and write. He also served as the primary carriage driver for the plantation. By the time his master moved his operation to Edgefield in 1861, he was known as the best carriage driver in the area. He was so good, in fact, that one day he stole his master's horse and went riding off the plantation to freedom. Somehow he managed to ride through Confederate Army lines, head for the coast, and join the Union Army's First South Carolina Loyal Colored Volunteers back in Beaufort.

We don't know his given name, but following escape and for the rest of his life, he was known as "Prince Rivers," a name he apparently gave himself. Though Blacks, even in a primarily Black unit, could not become officers in any branch of the American military, Rivers did reach the allowable noncommissioned rank of sergeant during his three military years. But his commander, Colonel Thomas Higginson, considered him more capable than his White soldiers and thought he should have been a commissioned officer instead.

How convenient for Rivers that, before the war ended, the Colored Volunteers had been sent to his former hometown of Edgefield, and how easy it was after the war for the now freed Sgt. Rivers to take off his uniform and join the new settlement of freedmen in nearby

Hamburg. Also, how fortunate it was for that new community when Rivers's now civilian status rose far above that of his military career. The more we learn of his postwar life, the harder it is to imagine how the town could have prospered as well as it did without all the roles he played in service to them.

As Registrar of Edgefield County in 1868, he was their delegate to the state constitutional convention. Within a few more years, he also became Hamburg's mayor and trial justice, representative to the state legislature, a general in the state militia at Hamburg, and a member and trustee of the town's Providence Baptist Church. In 1871, Rivers and two other prominent area freedmen—Speaker of the South Carolina House Samuel Lee and future Aiken postmaster Charles Hayne—were the founders of Aiken County, the only new South Carolina county to be formed during Reconstruction, which now encompasses the town of Hamburg.

As we can see from the previous paragraph, the Fifteenth Amendment had a spin-off. Besides granting the newly declared US citizens the right to vote, the freedmen could now enter politics themselves, and they did. Along with Rivers and House Speaker Lee, by the year 1873, more than half the seats in the state legislature were held by Blacks.[49] But if you thought the war, emancipation, and the other amendments were controversial, you haven't seen anything yet.

What a firestorm this perceived political imbalance created across the South, especially in the town of Hamburg. It wouldn't be a trade war this time, or a struggle between neighboring states. Politically and racially, it would be much worse.

CHAPTER 33

The Plan

Mercifully for the understaffed, underfunded, and minimally successful Freedmen's Bureau, Congress dismantled their operation in the summer of 1872. However, several other primarily northern groups also "came to help." No one sent them. Teachers, ministers, businessmen, and others with a variety of skills offered their services to war-recovering Whites and Blacks alike. But their motives were questioned. These were not saviors, folks said, but opportunists. Most stayed until they, too, were discouraged or sent away. Since they hadn't intended to stay long anyway, they arrived with few belongings in handheld bags made from carpet material, leading to the name "carpetbaggers," by which they've been known ever since.

One group, however, had a different objective. Rather than concentrate on the South's material needs, these "helpers" were more interested in their thinking, especially their politics. They called themselves Republicans. Political opponents added the word "radical" before their name. Although the traditional White Democrats desperately wanted this group to go away too, the new Black voters welcomed them, learned from them, and, in large numbers, registered as Republicans because of them. Soon Hamburg became known as a South Carolina Republican stronghold.

Talk about adding insult to injury. The South had just lost a war, their entire way of life was uprooted, and now all their perceived class distinctions had been turned upside down as well. For as long as anyone could remember, White men had been their leaders in every way. In politics, make that *Democratic* White men. And now, more than just being equal citizens, some of the very people over whom they had towered for so long were holding sway over them.

This was too much, and it would not be tolerated. In South Carolina, Martin W. Gary and Matthew C. Butler, both former Confederate generals and current Edgefield attorneys, along with a young protégé named Benjamin Tillman, would see to that.

Fortunately for Gary and company, if not for the new status quo, in January 1876 he received a letter from a Mississippi planter describing that state's success in resolving this very issue. Following the mantra "The end justifies the means," the Mississippi plan advocated using any and all means necessary to achieve their passionately desired end, redeeming the South to her former state of White supremacy. What better time to adopt such a plan than now? It was 1876, an election year, and these three, plus a host of the like-minded, lost no time in putting their "South Carolina plan" into action.

Steps along redemption's way began by making every effort possible to reduce Black voting. Their methods might include stuffing ballot boxes, interrupting campaign events, and closing voting precincts near Black homes and opening others farther away or in locations that were difficult to find. If these methods were not sufficient, they would then resort to threats and intimidation, even going so far as to place armed men near their precincts to frighten potential voters away.

But the one means redeemers found most promising was to observe the Black communities, study their habits and schedules, and watch for an incident or, if necessary, provoke one—something they could turn into an altercation between the races. Having been schooled in the recent war, these former soldiers and commanders had no doubt they would have the upper hand should such an event occur.

Five years earlier, in 1871, the state had established a militia in Hamburg. More akin to today's National Guard than an army prepared for battle, this lightly-armed, all-Black group varying from fifty to eighty strong might be called on to handle a domestic disturbance or to provide aid and order during a natural disaster. But Gary, Butler, and especially Tillman were confident they had access to an even better White counterpart to the militia's official operation.

Although the Ku Klux Klan had been founded immediately after the war for the very purpose of upholding White supremacy, its members were more active in or near their founding state of Tennessee and scarcely made an appearance in South Carolina. They also were not well organized at the time, leading, at least temporarily, to their nearly fading from existence by 1876.[50]

But South Carolina and nearby states already had a number of well-organized and very popular rifle clubs. Also called saber clubs or paramilitary groups, in South Carolina alone there were at least twenty thousand experienced and well-armed members of these clubs. With such a ready defense, a confident M. C. Butler found it amusing when Congress considered sending a paltry one thousand new troops to quell continued unrest in the state. Still, he and the others were quite sure their own arsenals would be necessary as their plan went into operation. As Gary was heard to say, "One ounce of fear is worth a pound of persuasion." Tillman, leader of the Sweetwater rifle club in Aiken, was even more explicit: "Nothing but bloodshed and a lot of it could answer the purpose of redeeming the State from Negro and Carpet Bag rule."[51]

CHAPTER 34

The Incident

White parents have White sons, of course. And after years of parental influence, example, and general way of life, all that additional family resemblance becomes equally obvious. Unlike beauty or outward appearance, however, those absorbed traits run more than skin deep.

Edgefield farmer Robert J. Butler had a twenty-two-year-old son named Tommy, and fellow townsman George E. Getzen had a slightly older son named Henry, who happened to be married to Butler's daughter. By July 4, 1876, coincidentally the date of the country's first centennial, these two young brothers-in-law were on their way to becoming full-fledged replicas of their White supremacist elders.

Tommy and Henry were well-acquainted with Hamburg, having visited often or traveled through when delivering Mr. Butler's crops to market in Augusta, and Hamburg was well-acquainted with them. "Rowdies" they and their youthful counterparts were called, for their whooping and galloping, ignoring signs and rules, or just being a nuisance—especially to Hamburg marshal Jim Cook, who more than once fined them both for their behavior. But on that national celebration day, these two were just the ones to help set the South Carolina redemption plan in motion.

It may or may not have been because of the holiday that Hamburg Militia captain Dock (or Doc) Adams, made certain plans for the day. He would take his company out to their accustomed site on Market Street along the river and march up and down that thoroughfare between Hamburg and the bridge to Augusta for one of their frequent readiness drills. Some forty men, or about half the membership, were on hand that day for the exercise.

Tommy Butler and Henry Getzen were out for the day too, but not to march in any parade. Their outing had another purpose. Earlier on that Tuesday morning, they had driven their horse and buggy to Augusta. Later, after crossing the bridge on their return home, they noticed the parade and stopped beside the road to watch. Devilment may also have been on their minds—part of the rowdiness for which they were known.

But this was more than horseplay. They knew about their father's redemption plan. They also may have known about the parade. Likely, the trip itself was planned. Before long, they stopped watching and made their move.

As the militia turned and marched back toward the pair, Butler and Getzen moved their buggy onto the road, quickened the horse to a trot, and drove directly into the militia's path. Realizing the danger, Adams ordered his men to halt. The buggy also stopped, and the altercation, in words similar to the following, began.

"Let us through!" Butler and Getzen demanded.

An astonished Adams replied, "This road is 150 feet wide, and we are only four men deep. Why are you interrupting an official military drill when there's plenty of room for you to go around?"

"Oh, not me!" Getzen protested. "I *always* go through the middle of the road because that's where the ruts are, and that's better for the horse and the buggy."

Butler's objection was even more testy: "This is my Daddy's road!" he shouted, pulling rank, perhaps, by drawing on his father's reputation as a prominent area planter. Never mind that neither they nor "Daddy" were making a market delivery just then, but merely returning home in an empty buggy.

Reluctantly, but realizing the potential for further trouble with the young men, Adams ordered his men to separate into two columns and allow the buggy, horse, and riders to proceed, as requested, through the middle of the road. The confrontation was over in minutes. End of story, right? Hardly.

Search and you shall find many reports of this and related events—everything from newspaper articles and official reports at the time to book chapters, academic theses and, of course, hearsay, published throughout the twentieth century and even to the present day. Predictably, you'll also find opposing points of view, including far more defensive or disparaging language, depending on which side is doing the writing or the telling. But the basic event, whether planned or otherwise, remains very much the same. The militia *were* parading on that public street. The two White men *did* watch for a while and then drive toward the group and demand to be given the right of way. And Adams and company eventually *did* what they were asked to do. But despite the apparently peaceful end to their disagreement, what happened on Hamburg's Market Street on July 4, 1876, was little more than an introduction to the incident the White supremacists had been longing for all along and would exploit to their advantage in the coming days.

The next day, Wednesday, July 5, R. J. ("Daddy") Butler was in the buggy with his son and son-in-law when they returned to Hamburg to talk with Trial Justice Prince Rivers. Tommy and Henry related what happened to them the day before, and R. J. demanded punitive action against Dock Adams. The captain's crime? Obstruction of a public thoroughfare. Butler's hypothetical reasoning? Besides inconvenience, he likely meant, "What if we had been driving a wagonload of fresh produce?" Didn't Rivers realize what a delay could have done to his crops?

In addition to his judicial duties, Rivers also served as general of the militia. Thus, he had two options for finding out what happened on Market Street the day before. If Adams had acted wrongly in his military role, Rivers or another of his superiors would need to bring the captain in for a court-martial. Otherwise, if the incident were a civil matter, Rivers could handle the situation in his judicial role. But first he needed to talk with the accused himself. So he summoned Adams to face his accusers and give his side of the story.

Adams had become militia captain only a couple of months earlier, but when he assumed the position, he decided to increase their number of readiness drills from the sporadic once every month or so to once or twice a week. Did that mean he and his men were a frequent public nuisance and needed to be dealt with anyway? Probably not, for the following reasons.

Market Street may not have been completely smooth over all its 150-foot width, but there were grassy or otherwise passable areas on at least one side for its entire length. Hamburg was also a small town. Thus, except for the Butlers and other farmers who now and then drove their produce to Augusta, few people at the time would have had the means or the need to use the road except for foot or single-horse traffic. Also, had there been earlier incidents like this one, Rivers certainly would have known about them and dealt with the captain before this.

Now assembled in Rivers's courtroom for a hearing, Adams and Getzen gave decidedly different accounts of the same event. Besides the blocked road, Getzen said he saw the men loading their guns and was afraid he and his brother-in-law were going to be shot. Adams countered by saying the men may have had guns for drilling purposes, but they did not have ammunition. He also said he and the militia had respected the young men, and moved out of the way in a matter of minutes so the buggy and riders could pass through as they wished. Adams, at least, didn't see what the fuss was all about.

He also didn't know much about court procedure. Thus, as tempers rose on both sides, and Adams kept interrupting when the others were being questioned, Rivers arrested him for contempt of court, ordered him to return for trial three days later, and adjourned the hearing. The town constable explained to the baffled Adams what the contempt charge was for and schooled him on procedures for Saturday's trial. A contrite Adams said he didn't know much about the law and apologized for his behavior.

We, too, may be baffled at why, of all possible outcomes, Adams was arrested for his actions in the courtroom rather than for what happened the day before. But after determining this was a civil matter and not a military one, Rivers's judicial decision toward Adams was more strategic than punitive. He and Adams were Black, the plaintiffs were White, and tempers all around were red hot. Rivers was well aware of the racial hostility in his town, and he knew those tempers needed time to cool off before a trial could be held. Above all, his mission was to protect the citizens of his town should this incident escalate further.

Unfortunately, three days would not be nearly enough time for these tempers to cool off.

CHAPTER 35

The Militia and the Mob

To accommodate those with daily chores, including himself, Rivers set the time for Saturday's trial at four o'clock in the afternoon. But farmer Butler and the others had far more on their minds that day than tending crops. More likely, their pretrial chores started the minute they left Rivers's office three days before. One such task for R. J. Butler was to hire the best attorney he knew, M. C. Butler, a former Confederate general, to represent them at the trial.

"Butler"? Were the attorney and the farmer related? Perhaps, although Edgefield was full of Butlers at the time and the exact relationship of the two men is not known. But one thing is certain: before this week ended, these two men would be blood brothers in action, if not in family.

By early afternoon on Saturday, or well before time for the trial, the plaintiffs, their attorney, and a growing number of armed White men were already in Hamburg. Acting more like the general he once was than a civilian attorney, M. C. Butler wanted the trial justice to know *his* plan for the day. Without divulging that the complaint against Captain Adams earlier in the week had only been the means—the provoked incident—behind the White supremacists' real intent, getting rid of the militia altogether, Butler told Rivers he wanted those men to surrender their guns to him that day. Then he would send them back to the governor where they belonged, rather than leave the guns in the hands of a Black militia who, his people believed, never should have had them in the first place.

Rivers had noticed the droves of armed men filling the streets of his town, many clad in their rifle club's red shirts, and now he knew the reason why. Alarmed, but hoping to prevent the carnage he knew was possible, instead of opposing Butler's unreasonable demand, he had another idea for getting the guns away from the militia. If Butler would let *him* collect the guns, he would return them to the governor himself. To him, that was a much safer way of handling the exchange—but not to Butler, who continued to insist that the guns be surrendered to him. Still, when Rivers asked Butler and the others to hold off on any confrontation with the militia until he had time to talk with Adams first, Butler did agree to the delay.

Meanwhile, during the interchange between Butler and Rivers, activity was also stirring within the militia. The warm day, combined with open windows and close proximity between homes and streets in the town, made it easy for Adams to overhear some very disturbing comments from the gathering crowd. Which is why, after hearing "We can't wait to take care of that militia captain" and similar threats, Adams told Rivers he would not be attending the trial because of fear for his safety. Rivers understood and told Adams to use his own judgment.

Part of that judgment included Adams's next decision. For extra precaution, he, along with some twenty-five to thirty members of the militia and a few nonmilitia Blacks, would leave their homes and go into the Sibley Building, a large brick warehouse nearby that housed their armory and drill room on the second floor. Now, following his meeting with Butler, Rivers hastened to the Sibley Building to have that talk with Adams.

He began by explaining what the consequences might be if the militia did not surrender their guns to Butler. Adams fully realized what could happen, but he also knew the rules of the militia. The state had established the company, Adams was their assigned captain, and the guns were his responsibility. Therefore, it would be illegal to transfer the guns to anyone who did not have proper authority to receive them, which included Butler and Rivers. If someone who did have authority requested the guns, Adams said, he would give them up. But, he emphasized, that would not be Butler. He also refused to meet with the attorney himself or to consider abdicating his responsibility regarding the weapons.

Rivers returned to Butler and the others to report on his talk with Adams. R. J. Butler, who seemed less militant than the attorney, offered a new solution. If the militia apologized for their insult to his son and son-in-law, he would make no further charges. But, he added, the matter was in the hands of his attorney, and the decision was up to him. Apology or no apology, that was not the decision M. C. Butler had in mind, especially after Adams refused even to discuss the matter with him. Rivers then asked the attorney whether he could guarantee the safety of the town should the militia surrender their arms. In addition to their paramilitary work, the militia also served as a kind of police presence for the town. Butler said that would depend on how the men behaved themselves afterward.[52]

Now Rivers had a decision to make, and that was to cancel the trial. After sensing what was about to happen, he also decided to gather his family and leave town, perhaps to Aiken, out of fear for their safety. In any event, as we'll find out later, he did not join the militia in the Sibley Building, and he did not go home.

By now the afternoon was over and evening well underway. But trial or no trial, everyone who had come to Hamburg that day either to observe or to help facilitate "the plan" was still there, and acting General M. C. Butler was still in charge.

Earlier, as those final and futile negotiations between Rivers and Adams were going on, an estimated 150 to 200 armed riflemen had positioned themselves along the street by the river, up to and partially around the Sibley Building. Butler then sent word to Adams that if the guns were not surrendered in half an hour, his people would take them by force. Another warning came fifteen minutes later.

Inside the building, the militia barred the windows and doors and retreated to their upstairs room. Anticipating an assault, Adams told his men not to fire until he gave the signal. Knowing they were outnumbered and outgunned, the company must have pinned hopes for survival on their marksmanship and the walls of the barricaded building they were sheltered behind. Soon Butler's announced time was up.

Armed Whites, standing between the abutment of the railroad bridge and the Sibley Building, fired first. Adams and company, crouching below the upstairs windows, returned fire. The first casualty occurred almost immediately, not from the building, but near the river. One of the White attackers, rifle club member McKie Meriwether, was shot through the head and instantly killed. Now, in rage and retaliation for the unexpected killing of one of their own, the riflemen continued firing nonstop for another half hour.

By this time, Butler realized they needed additional firepower, so he sent to Augusta for a cannon to be brought to the scene. Along with the artillery, another company of armed and eager rifle club members, this time from Augusta, crossed the river too. The cannon might accomplish what their handheld weapons could not do— damaging the building—and the extra men would reinforce the fight.

After four artillery charges, the door and every window in the front of the building had been shattered, and some of the beams inside reduced to splinters. Although there still were no casualties among the militia, the blasts had removed any protection the barricades might have provided. Even worse, they also were out of ammunition. They waited for Adams's next signal.

Before long the moon would be full, but it was still dark when Adams told the men it was time to leave the building. Without ammunition or barricades, they would have little protection should their attackers storm the building. Because there were no steps between floors at the rear of the building, the men used makeshift ladders to scale down from the second floor and escape through the back door. Adams told them to scatter, hide in cellars or under buildings, or run to any place where they could find shelter. Their exit came none too soon.

Besides guns (and plenty of them), some of the riflemen also carried axes, hatchets, and similar implements with which to further damage the building or, had they still been inside, to harm the occupants. But, as Adams expected, when the attackers did reach the building, they were surprised to find it empty. With a head start and under the captain's direction, several of the militia and others, including Adams, did get away, but McKie Meriwether would not be the only man to die that night.

CHAPTER 36

The Massacre

For nearly 150 years, whenever the subject of Hamburg, South Carolina, has come up, people have debated whether what happened there during the night of July 8, 1876, was a riot or a massacre. A careful comparison of the meanings of these two words should help us decide which one more nearly describes what everyone does agree was a terrible event.

Almost any dictionary or thesaurus equates "riot" with "disturbance, uprising, melee, brawl, or turmoil," while synonyms for "massacre" include "bloodbath," "genocide," "indiscriminate killing," "slaughter," and "ethnic cleansing." Though we often use "massacre" to describe a large number of casualties, the word can also be equated with "intensity" or "brutality." That's why, if by Sunday morning, July 9, Ben Tillman's prediction that "bloodshed and lots of it might be necessary to teach the black race a lesson" (see chapter 33) had come true, what happened that night can certainly be called a massacre.

Hours passed, including midnight, and the attackers still had not achieved their goal. Even after a barrage of gun and artillery fire, as far as they knew, the only casualty had been one of their own, and not one militia weapon was yet in their hands. But they were not giving up. Storming the building had been the first step. Finding it empty, they believed, did not necessarily mean all the occupants had time to leave the area. With the aid of a now full moon, they, as well as those in hiding or within earshot, knew the advantage had shifted to their side.

Besides the moon and lack of ammunition, the militia now had no one to whom they could signal their next move. Each man had to fend for himself. Adams realized their chances of survival would be greater if they did not all camp together in one group. Still, when the armed men stormed out the back of the building, they found those hiding places too.

The first man killed was Marshall James Cook, much to the delight of Tommy Butler and Henry Getzen, both of whom were said to have been the assailants. Moses Parks, another non–militia member, also died there about the same time.

As the hour approached 2:00 a.m., rather than continue the killings sporadically or on sight, the next twenty-five or more caught or routed from their hiding places were taken to an area near the railroad bridge designated as "the dead ring." There, guarded by a large company of armed men, some would be selected at random or, like Marshall Cook, recognized and singled out for retribution. The captives were no longer armed.

Prominent citizen Allen Attaway, one of Hamburg's commissioners who also served as a lieutenant in the militia, was the first man pulled from the ring. Despite his pleas and those of his mother who stood nearby, he was shot multiple times by members of the armed crowd.

Three more men from the militia—David Phillips, Hampton Stevens, and Albert Myniart—were next, each taunted or interrogated and then shot dead. Several others—including Pompey Curry, who recognized Henry Getzen in the crowd and begged him to spare his life, and Nelder Parker—were shot in the back and wounded after being told they could leave. Curry did recover, but Parker would later die and become the seventh Black person killed in the massacre. Another Tillman prediction had come true. Following Meriwether's death he said, "It would take more than two black killings to make up for the death of a white man."[53]

Was that it? When the remaining prisoners were allowed to run or limp away wounded, did the Butlers, Getzen, Tillman, and the rest declare their mission accomplished? Well, not quite yet. We have no record of further fatalities that night, but despite their full day of preparation and a battle lasting from sundown to nearly sunup, sleep could wait. It was time to celebrate.

Earlier on the now preceding day, in his ongoing effort to protect the town, Rivers had sent word to every merchant who sold liquor to close up shop and not let anyone buy alcohol that day. If he couldn't prevent the attack, he could at least try to limit the outcome. As far as he knew, his order was obeyed.

But the celebrating riflemen weren't about to let a few locked doors spoil their fun. Still armed with axes and other tools of demolition, they added a postscript to their night of terror by breaking into those liquor stores, consuming the contents, and turning their now drunken violence into a destructive melee all over town. Homes, warehouses, other shops—any buildings they could force their way inside—were ransacked, pilfered, and left in disarray. Between break-ins they tore down signs, cut ropes to the town's wells, leveled fences, and created havoc with whatever else their whims and weapons found to do. (It sounds as if there was a Hamburg riot that night after all.)

A couple of break-ins the rowdies may have especially enjoyed happened at the homes of Captain Adams and Trial Justice Rivers. As Adams would later testify, "They took down my pictures, broke up my furniture, broke up everything I had in the world. They took all my clothes, my mattresses, cut up my feather-bed in pieces and scattered it everywhere. I didn't have a suit of clothes left, only what I had on my back."[54]

At Rivers's house, they broke down doors, destroyed his papers, stole his and his wife's clothing, and took or damaged furniture. Had they not been stopped by some in their own group, they likely would have burned the house down.

In both cases, it could have been worse. Adams had found a secure hiding place, or he also may have gone to Aiken, and he did escape the worst devastation of all—losing his life. And Rivers? Without his own precaution, had he returned home after canceling Adams's trial, he, too, might have raised the night's death toll by one more.

When tiring of their celebration, some of the rowdies stopped at the Getzen house on the outskirts of Hamburg, feasted on fresh watermelon, bade Henry a good night, and went on to their own homes. In parting, ever the spokesman, Tillman declared himself satisfied with their strenuous day's work.[55]

CHAPTER 37

Did You Hear What Happened in Hamburg?

"Ghastly" is how witnesses described the streets of Hamburg the next morning. Gone were the crowds: the gunmen, the merrymakers—all but the curious or the courageous. But death remained, accompanied by the sounds of sobbing as bodies, lying where they had fallen, were identified. Constable William Nelson, who had narrowly escaped becoming a victim himself, came out of hiding and helped place the dead in coffins. Dock Adams came out of hiding too, but he stayed low, lest remnants of those who had hoped to do him harm were still on the hunt.[56]

Prince Rivers had no intention of remaining in hiding but returned from Aiken early in the day to survey conditions in the town and impanel a jury for a coroner's inquest. Two days later, after examining evidence and soliciting a great deal of testimony, he issued warrants for eighty-seven men, including M. C. Butler and Ben Tillman. By the time Rivers's findings and the results of a second inquest were transferred to the Aiken County sheriff, the number of men indicted had risen to ninety-four. Tommy Butler and Henry Getzen were among the seven charged with first-degree murder; the rest were charged as accessories before the fact.[57]

Governor Daniel Chamberlain, who also wanted to know what happened the night of the massacre, sent his attorney general, William Stone, to Hamburg to find out.

Arriving as Rivers's inquest was coming to a close, Stone interviewed the trial justice, spoke with a number of the wounded and other witnesses, and sent a detailed report to the governor with these conclusions:

- The demand on the militia to give up their arms was made by persons without lawful authority to enforce such demand or to receive the arms had they been surrendered.
- The attack on the militia to compel a compliance with this demand was carried out without lawful excuse.
- After there had been some twenty-five prisoners captured and completely in the power of their captors, five of them were deliberately shot to death, and three others severely wounded.
- Not content with thus satisfying their vengeance, many of the crowd added to their guilt the crime of robbery of defenseless people, and many were only prevented from arson by the efforts of their own leaders.

Stone does say there may be "some slight errors" in his report, a disclaimer that may have applied to the number of casualties, which was uncertain at the time.[58]

News of the big incident in the small town of Hamburg made headlines for weeks, not only locally and throughout the South but also across the North. Unlike Rivers and the governor, however, from both racial and political tradition, the news media was known to rely primarily on White sources for their information. Although Chamberlain and his attorney general were White, they also were Republicans, and at the time, politics trumped even race. Add another tradition that, during slavery and into the Reconstruction era, Blacks were at first forbidden and then afraid to testify or offer their opinions in public or print, and we have some idea of the tone and content of those published reports.

The nearby *Augusta Chronicle* (then known as the *Augusta Chronicle and Sentinel*) was the first to arrive in Hamburg that

Sunday morning to gather information for their readers. Thanks to Aiken author Isabel Vandervelde and her 1999 book *Aiken County: The Only South Carolina County Founded During Reconstruction*, we have a summary of the *Chronicle*'s coverage that week, including the excerpts below.

In Monday's paper, under headlines including, "WAR OF THE RACES" and "PITCHED BATTLE IN HAMBURG," reporters outlined what happened from the day of the buggy incident, "as two white men were detained on the street by a colored militia," to the final night, "when one white man and several Negros were killed." Readers learned about M. C. Butler's demand for the militia's guns, Rivers's unsuccessful efforts to persuade the militia captain to give in to that demand, and then Butler's determination to "accomplish by force, what could not be done by peaceable means." No names were listed for "the seven prisoners, considered ring leaders of this disturbing element in the County, who were fired upon and killed."

Tuesday's headlines, "ALL QUIET IN HAMBURG" and "INVESTIGATION NOT CONCLUDED" among them, indicated there was more to this story and details would follow. One man who desperately wanted his story told was the Augusta owner of the cannon used in the assault. He had no idea it was his weapon, he said, until he saw the forced-open gate of the cage where it was stored, nor would he ever have given permission for it to be used for such a terrible deed, as claimed by those who rolled it across the river. The obituary for young McKie Meriwether also appeared in Tuesday's paper.

But by Wednesday, July 12, a new element had crept into the Hamburg story: comparison and criticism among competing newspapers. Under that day's *Chronicle* headline, "THE HAMBURG TROUBLES," readers might wonder whether the headline instead should have read, "The Hamburg Reporter's Troubles," as indicated by the following: "We will publish tomorrow a full and truthful account of the Massacre at Hamburg. The details printed today are, of course, colored to suit the tastes of the murderers of unresisting prisoners." Then comes a clear disclaimer: "The above is from Governor Chamberlain's organ, the *Columbia Union Herald*, claiming to have copied its account of the massacre from the *Augusta Chronicle-Sentinel*." Then, in what sounds more like an editorial than a report, the writer insists, "The accounts that appeared in this paper have not been colored to suit the tastes of any person or class. They have been the plain and truthful narratives of a very unfortunate occurrence, and our reporter's information came from either what he saw or from eye-witnesses."

Now this or another writer seems to shift directions: "While we have nothing but condemnation for the murder of prisoners, we are not disposed to censure too rashly the determination of the White people in Edgefield County to disarm colored militia companies—not that we are against colored militia companies. The one in Augusta has not given anyone cause of offense; it is peaceful and law-abiding. But conditions are different in South Carolina, especially in Edgefield and Aiken Counties where the colored militia are simply political machines, mere tools in the hands of unscrupulous men to do irreparable mischief ...."

On another page in the same day's paper, under the headline "GENERAL BUTLER'S DEFENSE," the famed—or defamed— general complains angrily about how he has been portrayed and gives his explanation of what really happened:

"Certain reporters have done me much injustice with false reporting. I was told that the Negro militia threatened to lynch Tommy Butler and Henry Getzen if they were not convicted, and that's why the armed white men were there ... It was sort of a spontaneous combustion, a culmination of the system of insulting white people which the Negros had adopted for years ... Many things happened that night which cannot be justified, but the Negros sowed the wind, and reaped the whirlwind.

"But I have no idea of permitting reporters, for the sake of sensation, to present me as the leader of a mob. I was no more a leader, no more responsible than any other person who might have been there that night."[59]

Other papers also suffered rebuke. The editor of the *Charleston News and Courier,* for example, paid a heavy price for straying outside the lines of acceptable reporting in his coverage of what happened in Hamburg. After deploring the murders of the Negro militiamen "in cold blood after they had surrendered" and arguing that such goings-on could only hurt the Democratic cause, he found out soon enough how out of step he was with the prevailing view of the event.

First, his readers and advertisers boycotted the paper. Next, attorney and mastermind of the South Carolina plan, Martin Gary, challenged him to a duel "for saying such things about the Hamburg incident." Then, following passionate appeals in other press releases, "for white men of South Carolina not to desert their old General Butler, whether he had done right or wrong in Hamburg," the *News and Courier* editor apologized for "past condemnations of the Hamburg murders."[60]

Soon the *Anderson Intelligencer* joined the redeemed Charleston paper and others in a growing shift of opinion on who was to blame for the massacre. On August 10, scarcely a month later, the Anderson paper called Butler and all the other White men who had been accused in the Hamburg incident "men who belong to the best classes of society, (and) these charges touch the reputation of this section of law-abiding citizens." After regaling readers about "what they have been subjected to based on this one-sided testimony," the writer claims to have "new evidence from the most trusted sources, that completely rebuts the charges that the white men commenced the trouble ... The whole affair was an elaborate plan of the Negros and their radical leaders, and the killing of the prisoners was NOT participated in by the accused."[61]

In other parts of the country and further from the scene, sentiment fell largely on the side of the mistreated Blacks and against those who, most believed, were responsible for the killings. On August 12, the New York news magazine *Harper's Weekly* published an especially poignant political cartoon based on the Hamburg event. Drawn by the magazine's well-known cartoonist, Thomas Nast, the image depicts a gowned Lady Justice holding a very lopsided set of scales in her raised left hand. The much higher side contains the miniature body of one White man, while the heavier, lower side is piled high with six little Black bodies. The caption? "Five More Wanted," indicating what it would take for the scales of justice to be balanced.

In contrast, following debate on the matter in Congress, a Democratic senator from Mississippi rose to give his views. "Of course, such violence is terrible," he said. "But, in those southern states where it occurs, their governments are peculiar. Called Republican Governments, they encourage these disorders ... and in every instance, they fail to punish the murderers, and fail to administer justice or execute laws. Then they appeal to Congress or the North for help in maintaining the power they so ruthlessly exercise."[62]

As we know, this southern senator came from an already "redeemed state," where his once "peculiar government" had already been overthrown. Thus, it's not surprising that his sympathies lay closer to those of the South Carolinians urging support for "old General Butler" and his presumed wrongly accused associates than even the murderous violence he had just decried.

But soon the Mississippi senator, the South Carolina press, and the already large group of Butler supporters will further this unbalanced sentiment when the ninety-four men indicted in the Hamburg massacre appear before Aiken County Judge John Mayer on August 17, in preparation for trial before a grand jury at the upcoming September term of court.

CHAPTER 38

Justice on Trial

Didn't we just talk about a parade? At least that's what some called the drilling exercise Captain Adams scheduled for his militia back on July 4, before it became known as the incident that started the deadly massacre chain of events. But certainly no one would expect even the hint of a parade as that chain moved on to its next phase: bringing the perpetrators of the massacre to justice.

Though alternately called an inquest, a habeas corpus hearing, or a preliminary trial, none of these terms can be a synonym for "parade" by any stretch of a thesaural imagination—unless, instead of fearing their August 17 appearance before Judge Mayer, the ninety-four indicted men and their supporters marched into and around Aiken by foot or on horseback, fully confident of their upcoming vindication, and for the amusement of spectators along the way.

Ben Tillman's older brother George knew exactly what to do. Remembering a similar occurrence two years earlier in Mississippi, he urged the accused South Carolinians to "wear spectacular uniforms and parade their long procession of armed white men through the countryside ... Though assembled as prisoners, they should 'wave the bloody shirt' as a token of defiance."[63]

Sometime before their court date, brother Ben himself chaired the committee assigned to procure those uniforms. About half the men would still wear their customary rifle club red shirts, but with the help of Democratic Party authorities and a committee member who knew nearly all the ladies of Aiken, sufficient bolts of homespun cloth and seamstresses were found to make forty "spectacular" shirts for the occasion. The cloth itself was yellow, but with the aid of Venetian red dye, turpentine, and a few pokeberries, red splotches signifying bullet holes were daubed all over the now correctly designed "bloody shirts."

Then, to make the phrase "waving the bloody shirt," more applicable, one of the ladies created a giant-sized shirt for the men to place on a cross-shaped wooden frame, which was to be topped with an effigy of a Black man's head. This caricature, hoisted high like a flag, would then be carried by the leader of the planned procession. Recalling the reason for the Hamburg massacre in the first place, the unrepentant men on trial were still using any means possible to frighten Negros away from the voting booth, with the election now scarcely three months away.

Two days before their scheduled appearance, in order to finalize plans with the attorneys, the men from Edgefield made their way to Aiken. Attorneys? Yes, five in all, including two of the accused themselves—M. C. Butler and Martin Gary. Thanks to supporter William Shaw, who owned a plantation two miles west of town, they and the contingent from Aiken's Sweetwater rifle club were able to camp or occupy empty buildings there for the duration of the trial.

Court preparations consumed the early part of the next day, but by four o'clock in the afternoon the parade was about to begin. With horses ready and the flag bearer and bloody-shirted riders leading the way, the procession left the plantation and rode into Aiken. They moved quietly for a time, particularly past the homes of the ladies who had made their shirts. But at a given signal, the "bloody forty" broke away from the pack, stretched into a line nearly a quarter mile long, and galloped at breakneck speed through all the principal streets of the town. Clouds of dust kicked up by the horses on that dry summer day were no deterrent to the residents—men, women, and children—who lined the streets, waved handkerchiefs, and cheered as they raced by.

A half hour later, as energy but not enthusiasm waned, Tillman described how the parade came to an end: "Having shown how little terrified we were, we then proceeded to Coker Spring where we washed the dirt off our faces and out of our eyes and ears, watered our horses, and returned to our quarters." He couldn't help adding, "Not a Negro did we see." By all reports, the colored people of Aiken remained hidden indoors.[64]

Clearly, by the start of the next day's hearing, neither the little terrified mood of the assembled prisoners nor the size or amusement of the crowds had ended with the parade. As predicted days before by Aiken's *Courier-Journal*, "The event [promised] to be exceedingly interesting, attracting a large crowd, especially from Edgefield and the district about Hamburg."[65]

"Interesting" may not be how the officials would describe the day, however. Judge Mayer, for one; the sheriffs of Aiken and Edgefield Counties; Attorney General Stone and his assistants who represented the state—oh, and half the jurors—all must have recognized the seriousness of the day's proceedings and conducted themselves according to their assigned roles.

Half the jurors? Yes. Attorneys Butler and Gary were not the only participants working both sides of the case. The other six jurors were also among those on trial. Nevertheless, the bailiff called the court to order and the proceedings began.

Attorney Gary spent much of the day entering evidence in defense of the accused. More merriment ensued when he submitted 130 totally fraudulent affidavits offering elaborate alibis for the men, as well as claiming to have discovered a plan concocted by the dead

143

militiamen to kill the Whites. At the same time, as the day wore on, amusement mingled with concern whenever the defendants walked in or out of the room. All those shirts, whether red or bloody, were intentionally worn outside their pants, thereby hiding the sight but not the sound of their guns slapping against wooden benches whenever they left or returned to their seats.

On the prosecution side, given the gravity of the charges, Attorney General Stone asked the judge for $10,000 bail for each defendant. But the judge thought the reduced amount of $1,000 each would be sufficient.

What did the accused think of this decision? Since few of the men, rifle club members especially, had more than $100 to their name, let alone $1,000, the farce continued. When they asked the clerk about the process for filing their bonds, he said they could post them for each other. This, too, became a game when the poorest of the poor gleefully signed for thousands of dollars' worth of other men's bonds.

The hour was late, and by now court had adjourned. Frivolity still might have been the mood of the defendants, but fear had crept into the thinking of the officials. When one of the sheriffs heard the clerk tell the men they could come back and sign their bail bonds in the morning, he whispered, "You had better let these men get out of town tonight or else they may burn it down and hang you before morning."[66] That's when the clerk handed out blank bail bond forms, accepted their signatures alone, and let them leave the building. The sheriff knew there were far more armed men among the accused than there were of the authorities. Also, knowing what these men were being tried for, he likely wanted to make sure they all left town before another massacre or attack took place.

As Tillman summarized when relaying this information to his audience thirty-three years later, "In truth, the whole performance was in many respects a laughable travesty of law, for if they had attempted to put us in jail I am sure few or none of us would have acquiesced; and we would have probably killed every obnoxious radical in the courtroom and town, and gone to Texas or some other hiding place. In an hour we had departed and were on our way home."[67] Out on bail, their confidence high, and with time on their hands before the September trial, they had work to do. Without doubt, their primary focus would continue to be the looming 1876 election.

All this time, as Butler, Gary, Tillman, and the others were carrying out their plan to reduce Black voting, the Democratic Party had been busy preparing for the election too. But division had entered their midst. One faction felt their chances for victory would improve if they made alliances with Governor Chamberlain and other Republicans, in hopes of persuading some to align with Democratic causes.

But that would not be likely, claimed the larger "Straight-Out" faction, especially after those two former generals, Butler and Gary, not only joined forces with local party leaders but also managed to assume control of the Democratic Convention as well.[68]

For the next two months, they and hundreds of armed accomplices campaigned as if they were back on the battlefield. Tactics included disrupting Republican rallies, especially those of the undeterred Governor Chamberlain, who was running for reelection. But in every way possible, and with all the energy and torchlight parades they could muster, these men on a mission urged voters to elect the Democratic nominee, former Confederate war hero Wade Hampton III, to replace him. As for Hampton, he campaigned on a promise to reduce racial tension across the state, which he blamed on the Republicans.

But what about the September trial? What September trial? Unfortunately, what happened in Hamburg was not the only racial incident to occur during the run-up to the election, nor had the fear that gripped decision makers back in the Aiken courtroom subsided. Therefore, after realizing "no colored man would dare testify in court, and no jury would dare act," the attorney general ordered a continuation of the case in Aiken and told the grand jury not to proceed with indictments for the September term of court.[69]

With no mention of an October term of court, we can assume the September delay was simply repeated. Then, by November, all bets were off when Democratic nominee, Wade Hampton III, grandson of the state's wealthy, late-eighteenth-century planter, Wade Hampton I, won the South Carolina gubernatorial election.

Justice? What justice?

Hang on to your hats. We'll need another whole chapter to chronicle this development in South Carolina politics and wrap up the case against those ninety-four men accused in what, by now, was officially called "The Hamburg Massacre."

CHAPTER 39

𝔐onumental Results

No, the title of this chapter is not a reference to historic monuments, such as those gracing our landscapes and town squares today—at least not yet. Before then, with the aid of our handy thesaurus, we'll consider how many other ways this part of our story could be called "monumental" too.

Synonyms leap out at us: "Great," "enormous," "remarkable," or "tremendous" may be exchanged for the word "monumental," especially when some person, place, or event is remembered as grand, outstanding, unforgettable, or magnificent. But what if our subject is equally immense in size or effect yet is something we would rather forget than preserve in print, memory, or stone? What if it really is dreadful, shocking, unbelievable, or appalling? Then, too, the experts say, using the word "monumental" is entirely appropriate, albeit in a negative sense. For starters, perhaps "monumental" is just the word to describe the 1876 South Carolina election.

Wade Hampton may have won the governor's seat as far as Democrats and the numbers were concerned, but Republicans, crying fraud and intimidation, contested the results. Did they have a case? It certainly looked that way. Whether or not they could win their case in such a hostile political climate was not as certain.

Ben Tillman spent Election Day at his Edgefield County precinct until the votes were counted that night. He had to have been pleased with the tally for governor—211 to 2 in favor of Hampton—even if those not cheering said of the lopsided victory, "They didn't allow any colored men to vote."[70]

The same day found fellow poll watcher Martin Gary at the Edgefield County Courthouse, where not even attending US troops could remove two rows of armed Whites along the path to prevent Blacks from voting there. The courthouse was also where election results for the county would be known by the end of the day. First reports, in round numbers, were these:

- Democrats 5,500 votes
- Republicans 3,000 votes[71]

Monumental results? Absolutely, since the Democratic vote alone exceeded the number of White voters by three thousand, while total votes cast approached two thousand more than the number of voting-age men in the county, registered or not. (As a reminder, women could not vote until passage of the Nineteenth Amendment in 1920.)

By all accounts, the South Carolina Plan—stuffing ballot boxes and intimidating Blacks, along with incidents in Hamburg and elsewhere—had achieved a victory as well, at least in Edgefield County. But across the state, with overall election results much closer, Hampton won by only eleven hundred votes. Right away the Republicans believed they had enough evidence to prove Democratic fraud.

The proof was in the numbers—not just the vote tally but also in the racial breakdown between population and registered voters in the state. With the overall population at recognized Reconstruction-era levels, there were now nearly one hundred thousand more Black residents in South Carolina than Whites, and of that number, 36,500 more Blacks were registered to vote than Whites. Also, since all, or nearly all, Blacks were known to vote Republican at the time, had there been no voter intimidation, Republicans must have concluded, Chamberlain would have won in a landslide.

Not everyone paid attention to these findings. But the Republican-controlled state board of canvassers (board of elections today) were convinced of the fraud and declared the election results in Edgefield County and, for similar reasons, in Laurens County invalid. Without these two counties, Republicans retained their control of the State House of Representatives and assumed the authority to determine who had won the race for governor and other state offices.

In a countermeasure, after the Republican-controlled general assembly excluded members of the disputed counties from their body, the Democrats walked out in protest, reinstated the excluded members, and declared themselves a quorum. Then, brazenly perhaps, they returned to the statehouse, set up a rival legislature, and began conducting government business as if the Republicans were not doing the same thing in another room.

Meanwhile, a similar contest was taking place at the governor's mansion, where Chamberlain, believing the board's ruling retained him as the duly elected governor, refused to leave his office. And Hampton? Certified or not, he fully accepted the disputed vote tally, declared himself governor, and moved in as well. For the next four months, South Carolina had two functioning legislatures and two governors.[72] Talk about mixed messages. As for the rival governors, each man believed his was the final word in matters of executive authority. Thus, when Hampton decided to fire Prince Rivers from his duties as trial justice, Rivers appealed the decision to Governor Chamberlain, who told him, "You are to pay no attention to communications such as this from Mr. Hampton or his associates, but continue the functions of your office until further notice from this office."[73]

Still, as disturbing as this election was for the people of the state, what happened in South Carolina also affected the 1876 presidential election. That was the year the close race between Democrat Samuel J. Tilden and Republican Rutherford B. Hayes needed the unresolved electoral college results from South Carolina and three other states— Florida, Louisiana, and Oregon—before the presidency could be decided. In what is still called "one of the most disputed elections in American history," it also took four months that year before Americans knew who their next president would be.

When the national polls closed on Election Day, Tilden had won the popular vote by more than 250,000 votes, but that number assured him only of 184 uncontested electoral votes, or one short of a majority at the time in the electoral college. As for Hayes, his number in the electoral college stood at 163. To win the presidency, he would need all 22 of the disputed electoral votes, and Tilden only one. Oregon's problem, though settled quickly in favor of Hayes, appeared to be an in-house dispute over the party affiliation of one of the state's three electors. But in all three southern states, the conditions and objections were the same. With a larger percentage of Republican voters than Democratic, and a history of past Republican victories, each was considered a Republican state. Thus, when all three states suddenly went Democratic, the charge of widespread intimidation to reduce the Negro vote was leveled at all three.

Congress had a problem too. With a Republican Senate and Democratic House, their first attempts at resolving the conflict all ended in deadlock. Finally, near the end of January 1877, both sides agreed to a fifteen-member bipartisan commission comprising an equal number of Republicans and Democrats from each house of Congress, and an equally divided number from the Supreme Court, plus one independent from the court, chosen by the other justices.

A month later, after the independent justice voted with the Republicans, the commission awarded the returns from South Carolina to Hayes by unanimous vote and split eight to seven on the other two states, also in favor of Hayes. It was over. With the addition of all 22 disputed votes, Hayes now had enough electoral college votes to win the presidency—185 to Tilden's 184. The decision was made public on March 2, 1877, just three days before the inauguration of Rutherford B. Hayes as the nineteenth president of the United States.[74] (We should note that from George Washington in 1789 to Franklin Roosevelt's first term, all US presidents were inaugurated on March 4, unless, as occurred in 1877, the 4th was on a Sunday. With the adoption of the Twentieth Amendment in 1933, the March date was changed to January 20, where it has remained to the present day.)

Realizing his victory did not mean the entire country was suddenly on his side, President Hayes made several early concessions, particularly toward the Southern Democrats. At least they were happy when he removed those thousands of unwanted federal troops from their states, essentially allowing the southern people to settle their postwar problems by themselves without aid or interference from Washington. Also, this decision finally ended the largely unpopular movement known as Reconstruction.

If we were to call the new president's stance toward the southern states a "hands-off" policy, we would need to add that this was not a new idea concerning the division of responsibility between the federal government and the states. The recently convened bipartisan commission had been established only to settle the electoral college votes for the presidency, not to decide the election results within each state. To do so would have been an invasion of the sovereignty of the states, as defined in the Tenth Amendment to the US Constitution. Therefore, South Carolina still had an election to resolve.

As we can see, the 1876 South Carolina election had a direct effect on the race for president of the United States. But did the national election have a reciprocal effect on the state? Yes, but with that state sovereignty issue, it was perhaps not what we might expect. Although the state's vote tallies had been declared invalid by the Republicans, they were totally acceptable to the Democrats. An election with more votes than voters may have proven fraud to the Republicans, but the only proof the Democrats needed was that their candidates had received the most votes. Still, despite the presumptive actions of Hampton and the disgruntled Democrats during the months before the election was officially decided, Chamberlain had the presence of those federal troops to prevent the Democrats from simply ousting his administration and replacing it with their own. Now, with the troops withdrawn, the Republicans had no such protection.

Thus, with Hayes in and the troops gone, the Democrats lost no time in assuming control of the state government. Having already recertified the disputed Edgefield and Laurens County election results, they now expelled two dozen sitting Republicans to increase their majority in the legislature, replaced Republican attorney General William Stone with a member of their party, and, on April 11, 1877, declared Wade Hampton the official governor of the state.

A few weeks later, knowing he would have no federal help in maintaining his position, Governor Chamberlain read the proverbial handwriting on the wall, resigned from office, and left the state. Now, too, without Chamberlain's interference, in early June Governor Hampton dismissed Trial Justice Rivers for good and replaced him with a familiar name—that of rifleman and buggy driver Henry Getzen. The legislature also made some well-known appointments, including sending Martin Gary to the state senate and moving Matthew Butler a step higher to the US Senate.[75]

Speaking of familiar names, dare we ask what, if anything, has happened to that long-delayed trial for the ninety-four defendants in the Hamburg massacre? Yes, in time—several years, in fact—there will be an outcome. But other facts and outcomes need to be addressed first.

Soon after the election, based on their Senate Resolution of December 5, 1876, the Forty-Fourth Congress scheduled a lengthy hearing into the recent South Carolina election. Held at the state capitol in Columbia during the waning weeks of the year and into early 1877, this "Testimony as to the Denial of the Elective Franchise in South Carolina" examined certain events leading up to that election, including the July 4 incident preceding the Hamburg massacre. Among some three dozen witnesses for this part of the hearing were the participants in that altercation: militia captain Dock Adams and the two buggy drivers, J. T. "Tommy" Butler and Henry Getzen.

By now nearly six months had passed—time enough for memories to alter or intensify—but the basic claims were still the same. No, the captain said, he did not hinder or mistreat the other men in any way, beyond trying to settle the argument about use of the road, but he was full of complaints about how badly they had treated him. (See chapter 36.) As we might imagine, the other two had a far different tale to tell. In their minds, they were the mistreated ones—dangerously so, even to the point of fearing for their lives.

Although the full transcript of that hearing is still available in print, it provides no evidence that Congress took any action at the time either toward or against the participants in the buggy incident or in the resulting massacre. However, by the time a verdict is rendered in the massacre case, we know the federal government will be involved. Until then, occasional entries do appear, indicating that Governor

Hampton, or likely his new attorney general, repeatedly tabled the case, first from session to session and later from year to year.

Given all that upheaval between the massacre and the settling of the election, we have to wonder what life was like for the people of Hamburg during that critical time, or whether they even stayed? For the most part, they did not. Gradually, a majority of the town's Black citizens did leave, never to return. Gone was their postwar haven, and in its place a new leadership under whom they had good reason to believe they would be neither welcome nor safe.

Likewise, without his militia, and thus a purpose for remaining, Dock Adams left too. The family may have gone first to Augusta to live with his wife's mother, but they later moved to Aiken. Other than his testimony before the congressional hearing in December, little is known about the former captain's life or whereabouts from this time on. But we do have considerable information about Prince Rivers.

While the former trial justice, mayor, militia general, and overall involved citizen no longer held any prominent leadership position, after moving his family to Aiken, he continued to maintain a prominent presence there for the rest of his life. Still, although he was greatly admired by those he had served among, he also had his detractors, and some of them had long memories. Scarcely a year after the move, one of those memories resurfaced and, in a mastery of manipulation, clouded what might have been his well-deserved latter years.

In September 1878, Rivers and every former Black political leader of Hamburg, along with most White Republicans who stood with them, were indicted by the state for old charges of conspiracy and breach of trust with fraudulent intent. According to the evidence reported to them, the *Augusta Chronicle* attempted to put together the murky details.

Seven years earlier, their sources said, Rivers and the other named individuals had all been in on a scheme to receive kickbacks in the purchase of a new site for the Aiken County Courthouse. Then, when they settled on buying the old Gregg mansion, they agreed to pay Mr. Gregg's inflated price of $15,000, which was a good $5,000 more than the property was worth, and Gregg would give $3,000 back to them.

However, intentionally or not, neither the state nor the newspaper checked their sources against the word of Rivers or any of the ones charged. Otherwise, although there likely had been a conspiracy by someone, they would have learned that none of the accused were ever the recipients of that money. Instead, "Gregg's skillful agent thwarted the designs of the conspirators by sweeping the money into his own pocket." Though the "skillful agent" was not named, Gregg's attorney was known to be Martin Gary, currently a new state senator, who had been among the formerly accused in the Hamburg massacre, as well as one of their attorneys.[76]

Nevertheless, Rivers was convicted of the entire scheme. But, with a recommendation of mercy, he was allowed to post a $1,500 bond, pending an appeal. Though the case remained on the books year after year, there was never a trial. Finally, six years later, and with no explanation at the time, the case was stricken from the books.

Eventually there was an explanation—an astounding one. And, as unearthed years later by the *Charleston News and Courier*, the disposition in the Rivers case would have a strikingly familiar connection to another long-delayed judicial decision. To wit:

> With the enthusiastic support of U.S. Senator Matthew C. Butler, the United States Government agreed to drop the civil rights cases against the Hamburg murderers and all white rifle club members not prosecuted by the State for crimes in the 'Bloody Fall of 1876.' The price the Federal

Government asked was modest: that South Carolina drop all corruption charges against the Republican office-holders in the State for the Aiken County Courthouse conspiracy.

So, Prince Rivers was politically guillotined long before his case was finally dismissed in 1885.[77]

Perhaps now, with this appalling outcome to such a terrible event, we have reached the ultimate, monumental result.

As we gasp, wondering how such an unfair decision could have been reached, there may be at least one clue to explain why. Apparently Senator Butler had more to do with this decision than just to offer his "enthusiastic support." It may even have been his plan.

Back when Rivers was first charged, former attorney general William Stone sent a letter to Governor Hampton advising against bringing the Rivers group to trial because "the corruption charges would not stand the test of legal evidence." Instead, Stone said, "Publishing the charges but not going to trial would achieve the same thing without risking the backlash an acquittal or hung jury would cause."[78]

As we may recall, though he, too, was among the accused, Butler was also one of the defense attorneys in the massacre case, and one of his tactics also involved delay. "To keep a case from looking bad," he said, "wait a while, don't drop all charges at once or at the same time. The continuous process looks better."[79]

It was now 1885, seven years past the Rivers conviction, and nine years after the massacre. Considering the passage of time, the current attorney general had obviously taken his predecessor's advice about not bringing Rivers to trial right after he was charged. Now that he was the top legal officer in the state, and it would be his responsibility to rule on the massacre conspiracy proposal, he also had the benefit of this similar opinion by yet another attorney, the noted Senator Matthew Butler. It wouldn't take long. As reported at the time, "The State Attorney General was all for this plan."[80]

Three highly positioned legal minds, alone or together, were fulfilling the centuries-old adage "Justice delayed is justice denied."

For Rivers, whatever personal relief he felt over this decision must have been overshadowed by the knowledge that his acquittal was the "modest price" paid for dropping all charges against the ninety-four participants in the Hamburg massacre. His own dead townsmen, militia members, and friends had just paid a far higher price for this injustice, and their friends and family members would now have even more reason to grieve.

But whatever his morale, perhaps now Prince Rivers would finally have that much delayed time to enjoy his latter years. Sadly, time he would not have. Before long, he developed symptoms of the kidney-destroying Bright's disease, which confined him to his bed for months and, on April 13, 1887, at age sixty-five, claimed his life.

The reporter who wrote his obituary, thinking his eventful career as a colored man deserved more than a passing notice, made inquiry into a sketch of his life. That sketch turned into paragraphs of detail, from Rivers's beginnings as a slave to his escape and service in the Union Army, and then to his long and impressive political career in Hamburg and Aiken County, South Carolina.

By this time, even the reporter was impressed. After realizing this former town and county leader had spent several of those latter Aiken years as a common laborer, he closed the obituary with these poignant thoughts: "In point of intelligence, far above average; a darkey respected by whites and looked up to by his colored brethren with much reverence; and a trusted employee of the Highland Park

Hotel, where he served as a carriage driver, the same job he once held as a slave."[81]

Years later, in an article for the *Augusta Chronicle* about Aiken County, the town of Hamburg, and Prince Rivers in particular, reporter Jim Nesbitt included some admiring thoughts about Rivers from North Augusta pastor and educator Rev. Nathaniel Irvin Sr. Realizing that, among his other credentials, Rivers was also a cofounder of Aiken County, but knowing there was no visible reminder of the distinguished man anywhere in the county today, Irvin suggested how Rivers should be memorialized:

"I notice there are bridges and highways named for Jefferson Davis, the President of the Confederacy. I think Mr. Rivers' name should also be on a public edifice. Prince Rivers' name isn't highlighted anywhere, and it ought to be."[82]

We of the twenty-first century are well aware of other familiar nineteenth-century names that, while heralded by many if not by all, have been memorialized on bridges, highways, edifices, and in statues of stone. We'll close this monumental chapter by listing some of them.

Rifle club founder and White supremacist leader Benjamin Tillman went on to combine his success as a well-to-do planter with an even more renowned political career. His two primary emphases, bringing new agricultural technology to South Carolina and returning White supremacy to the political arena, propelled him into becoming one of the state's most prominent citizens during the latter nineteenth and early twentieth centuries. Thanks to his lobbying the general assembly for an agricultural college, and further influencing wealthy Thomas Green Clemson to help finance just such a school, Tillman is credited with founding Clemson Agricultural College in 1889. About the same time, because Clemson was then an all-male school, he also helped establish Winthrop College, a teacher training school for women. Each campus soon named one of its buildings "Tillman Hall."

But it wouldn't be his agricultural or educational pursuits for which Tillman was most recognized. Those efforts may have helped raise his public image, but it was his lifelong obsession with White supremacy that launched him into politics and kept him there for the rest of his life. As governor for two two-year terms—from 1890 to 1894—in the now solidly Democratic state, he had plenty of help authoring and passing what became known as Jim Crow laws and setting the stage for a new, revised South Carolina Constitution in 1895.

By explanation, "Jim Crow" was a derogatory term for "Negro," and by purpose, Jim Crow laws, in South Carolina and other former Confederate states, were enacted primarily to impose racial segregation in most public facilities, and certain defined circumstances, against the Black race.

Obviously, voting was a primary target. Despite passage of the Fifteenth Amendment, which gave all US citizens the right to vote regardless of race, these new laws added requirements and restrictions to that right, including literacy tests, poll taxes, property ownership, and removal from voter rolls after missing a previous election.

Of course, poor or illiterate Whites were affected by these new requirements as well, but the impact against them was minor in comparison. Not only were there fewer Whites in those categories, but grandfather clauses and other loopholes could often be found to release them from such laws. Thus, it wasn't long before the White supremacists had achieved their primary goal: disenfranchisement of the Negro voters. They would not fully recover the right until the national Civil Rights Acts of the 1960s.

But Tillman was still on the rise. He left the governorship in 1894 after being appointed to the US Senate to replace Matthew C. Butler, and he held that seat until his death in 1918. He also maintained his pride in helping redeem the state from "Carpet-Bag and Negro Rule" following the war. In fact, in his previously mentioned speech, "The Struggles of 1876," delivered at the Red Shirt Reunion in Anderson, South Carolina, in 1909, he credits that involvement as the reason he became a Senator fifteen years before. Butler, the former Confederate general, and literal general of the Hamburg event, always denied having any role in the massacre except for casual interest. Thus, we have to assume, in the minds of their constituents, Tillman's actions and admission were more "honorable" than Butler's denials.

Monumentally speaking, in addition to those two college buildings named earlier in his honor, on May 1, 1940, Benjamin Ryan Tillman's eight-foot bronze statue, mounted on a substantial stone pedestal, was unveiled on South Carolina's statehouse grounds in Columbia. The inscription on the east side reads in part, "THIS MONUMENT ERECTED BY THE LEGISLATURE, THE DEMOCRATIC PARTY, AND PRIVATE CITIZENS OF SOUTH CAROLINA." This monument and the Tillman name on those two now university halls still stand, in spite of calls by modern historians and growing public sentiment to have each one removed.

Reminders of Wade Hampton, as well as his tenure on the political stage, are less numerous than those of Ben Tillman. Still, Hampton also was elected governor for two terms before resigning midway through his second term when he was appointed to the state's other US Senate seat, where he would serve two complete terms from 1879 to 1891. A number of South Carolina streets and other locations, plus a county, town, and city park in North Augusta, are also named for Hampton, while his 1906 monument depicting the governor seated on horseback has stood on statehouse grounds, without controversy, for thirty four years longer than that of his political contemporary, Ben Tillman.

The final monument in our series, and likely the one stirring the most interest to history buffs and South Carolina citizens alike today, is the century-old, twenty-one-foot-tall obelisk honoring Thomas Mckie Meriwether, the lone White man killed that awful night in Hamburg. Standing prominently at the pinnacle of Calhoun Park in North Augusta, the city that now includes the former Hamburg site as part of her own, this monument is the epitome of what Clemson University graduate student Jenny Heckel calls "the white manipulated memory of the past."[83]

For nearly forty years, the idea for a Meriwether monument had been suggested by many, including US Senator Ben Tillman. But it would be a political newcomer, Edgefield's James P. DeLaughter Jr., who, following his election to the State House of Representatives in 1912, began putting action behind sentiment to create just such a monument. As the proud son of a Confederate soldier, DeLaughter believed honoring Meriwether in this way would serve as "an example of all the white heroes who sacrificed their lives during Reconstruction."[84]

Within a year, the freshman legislator's passion for the monument had achieved results. Before the end of 1913, the general assembly agreed with both the monument idea and DeLaughter's request for $400 to pay for it, and the Senate followed through by appointing a five-member commission to pursue and supervise the project. It would take more time and, as the commission soon realized, more money. But with one commissioner's suggestion to raise a matching $400 in public donations, plus an offer from DeLaughter's—and Meriwether's—hometown newspaper, the *Edgefield Advertiser*, to publicize and collect those funds, by early 1914 the resolution to request that original $400 from the state was ready for the governor's signature. But Governor Coleman Blease vetoed the resolution.

With such overwhelming support for the monument, why was the governor not on board? Could he have known the full circumstances of Meriwether's death and therefore been unwilling to pay him such an honor?

Nothing of the sort. If anything, Blease was a White supremacist to the extreme and was no friend of the Black race. Besides denying Negros the right to vote, he didn't want them to receive an education. Had he been more than a child at the time, he, too, might have taken part in the massacre.

No, the governor's objection was aimed entirely in another direction, at his long-time rival, Ben Tillman. The two men may have begun their political careers in much the same camp, but while Tillman catered to the interests of tenant farmers and wealthy planters, Blease turned his attention to a class of people he considered politically underrepresented—the rising tide of mill workers and sharecroppers. Other differences arose, too, as did their anger toward each other, especially after Tillman campaigned vigorously—and successfully—to defeat Blease's appointment to the US Senate. Otherwise, the governor might have led the charge for a Meriwether monument himself, if he hadn't known Tillman was one of its chief supporters.

Now, though DeLaughter's cause had grown from one man's idea to that of a majority of the legislature, Blease's counter cause had almost no support at all. Thus, after the governor signed his veto on the morning of March 5, 1914, the still passionate Edgefield legislator "gave his maiden speech on the House floor that very evening, urging his colleagues to override the veto. They did, overwhelmingly: 80 to 4."[85]

It still would take time—two more years, in fact—before the monument became a reality. But that time did not stand still. Before long, the commission chose the Owen Brothers Granite and Marble Works in Greenwood, South Carolina, to design and build the monument. In addition to its twenty-one-foot height, the Winnsboro granite structure would weigh twenty-seven thousand pounds and need time and space for lengthy inscriptions to be etched on all four sides.

Meriwether Monument.
(Bruce Wilson, photo)

One month shy of two years later, on February 16, 1916, local citizens and dignitaries from far and near unveiled the long-awaited monument dedicated to "the brave and patriotic young man, McKie Meriwether, whose life was immolated on his country's altar in July, 1876."[86] Daniel S. Henderson, by then the only surviving attorney who had represented the accused in the Hamburg massacre, delivered the keynote address, titled "The White Man's Revolution in South Carolina." Also honored, but notably missing, was the man whose unwavering efforts had culminated in this day. Not long after the March 1914, decision to proceed with the monument, James P. DeLaughter Jr. developed stomach cancer, and he died on January 14, 1915, a year and a month before his major legislative achievement became a reality.

The celebration, the tributes, and, most of all, those inscriptions on the monument were all reflections of the White supremacist social and political thinking of the post–Civil War era. Without this realization, those from a different time or who *do* know the full circumstances of Meriwether's death could not possibly understand why he was honored in such a monumental way. They also may not realize there were no monuments honoring Black men at that time or place—not even the victims of a massacre or the casualties of war. Jenny Heckel's "white, manipulated memory" idea is easier to understand, though still difficult to accept, when reading the inscriptions on the Meriwether Monument, including the following excerpts:

> In memory of THOMAS McKIE MERIWETHER who, on the 8th of July, 1876, gave his life that the civilization builded by his fathers might be preserved for their children's children unimpaired.
>
> In … the unfinished years of manhood … he accepted death, maintaining those institutions which the men and

women of his race had struggled through the centuries to establish in South Carolina.

In life he exemplified the highest ideal of Anglo-Saxon civilization. By his death he assured to the children of his beloved land the supremacy of that ideal.

Calhoun Park sits on public land in the heart of the city, allowing access to anyone who desires a closer look or complete reading of the messages on the Meriwether Monument. In recent years, many have taken that closer look, giving rise to a growing chorus of people who would like the monument removed because it no longer exemplifies local thinking or belief. Ongoing studies and steps already taken to answer these requests will be covered later, as we discuss the last days and legacy of the town once called Hamburg.

CHAPTER 40

Hamburg's Last Days

Hamburg, South Carolina, the town that Henry Shultz built, had a number of "last days"—and recoveries—during a full century of life. Within the first decade, financial missteps by many, including Shultz, threatened to close the town or cede control to the state. Somehow, agreements were struck several times over until, by 1835, Hamburg was known as the leading interior market of South Carolina. (See chapter 25.)

Then, in the 1840s, neighboring Augusta, whose own status as a leading market had been noticeably diminished by the new town across the river, succeeded in turning that diminishing designation back to Hamburg by removing tolls from the bridge they now owned and building the Augusta Canal. Free passage across the bridge pleased upstate patrons and lured them on to that larger market in Augusta. Also, because of the new waterway, boat traffic could reach the city without detouring through Hamburg to escape the dangerous Savannah River rapids. But the biggest diminishing at the time occurred when the South Carolina Railroad, whose predecessor's historic arrival had brought so much attention and prosperity to the town, began extending its tracks into the upstate region, and, in 1853, across the river into Augusta, thereby removing the need for travelers to pass through Hamburg or stop on the way. (See chapter 29.)

Could the town possibly recover after all this? Well, perhaps not to her former "leading market" days, but plenty of Hamburg's historic and somewhat prosperous days still lay ahead. Nevertheless, the loss of trade and traders, the death of Henry Shultz in 1851, and the advent of the Civil War a decade later reduced the size and purpose of the town to little more than a bedroom community for Augusta.

But, as we know, following the war, the nearly vacant town was just the right place for hundreds of newly freed slaves to begin their lives anew. Hamburg then experienced another surging, if tumultuous, revival. This time, however, when the tumult subsided and the chaotic days of the massacre were over, many of those new residents moved elsewhere. After all this, we would have to call the next few decades Hamburg's lingering, but decidedly final, days.

Until now, we've been speaking only of the town's residents, who lived there or moved away, and why. But the area itself, from the "old cornfield" to the "mighty Savannah River," also has a story to tell. Yes, the river was a tremendous resource—"nature's roadway" for traffic, trade, and transportation, and the primary water source to sustain life. But when the rains came, as they often did, and in unwanted amounts, it's hard to find a period longer than a decade or two when that great resource did not overflow its banks to a disastrous degree.

Floods were largely responsible for destroying all area bridges across the river until 1814, when Henry Shultz and Lewis Cooper mastered the combination of materials and design, and built "a bridge to last" (see chapter 3). And it did, for nearly seventy-five years. In the end, as Peter Hughes explains, "The structure was durable, but not indestructible. A third of its length was washed away during a flood in 1840, and half that much in another flood in 1852. Each time the bridge was quickly repaired, and remained in service until it was completely destroyed in the flood of 1888."[87]

The Shultz Bridge gone? This landmark had been in existence for seventy-five years; hardly anyone alive could remember a time when it wasn't there. Now, other than by train, small boat, or ferry, how would folks cross the river from one town, one state, to the other?

But the space of seventy-five years also allowed time for the art of bridge building to improve enough so that a common covered wooden bridge for foot and vehicle traffic could soon be erected in the same vicinity, reconnecting Hamburg to Fifth Street in Augusta. Still, when severe flooding returned, these bridges were also vulnerable to damage or loss and might need to be repaired or replaced. So, for a more permanent solution, could history repeat itself? Surprisingly, that's very nearly what happened next.

Another man, in many ways reminiscent of Henry Shultz, also had big dreams. Even as a child, Augusta-born James U. Jackson looked across the Savannah River and saw scenic hills instead of cornfields, but few signs of settlement during Hamburg's declining days, and wondered why someone hadn't built a larger town on that side of the river too. With maturity, education, and a foothold in the business world by his early thirties, Jackson became that "someone," and made plans for just such a town.

By 1889, this young man had already organized a brokerage firm, attracted northern capital, invested money and his own leadership in several area railroad companies, and formed the North Augusta Land Company. From these holdings, Jackson's Company was able to pay the $100,000 purchase price for fifty-six hundred acres in what was to become his desired town, also named North Augusta. The deed to this property was signed on March 24 of the following year.[88]

And what was priority number one for his new town? Would it be a home, an office, or streets and adjoining lots for settlement? All those categories were already in the planning stage, but James U. Jackson's first building project was a bridge.

Sound familiar? Like Shultz, Jackson knew that in order to attract people and business across the river, he had to make a way for them to get there. Yes, they could still use the Fifth Street Bridge and meander through the dwindling streets of Hamburg, but Fifth Street was some distance away from the Thirteenth Street location he had chosen to lead directly into the center of his town. Hence the need for Jackson's early 1891 meeting with the Augusta City Council to request—and receive—permission to build that very bridge. Also, in another important first, this bridge, which opened for public use in October of the same year, would be the area's first steel bridge, perhaps on the advice of his northern investors, who were accustomed to this modern and more durable bridge construction now common in other parts of the country.

Was it durable? For at least the foreseeable future, we might say, the Savannah River had no intention of mending its ways, and the flood that destroyed the Shultz Bridge three years before was by no means the last time the river's banks would overflow or bridges would be destroyed. Yet, in spite of these calamities, and except for some repairable damage after a couple of those floods, Jackson's steel bridge stood tall and serviceable for almost fifty years, or until replaced by the current, even sturdier concrete bridge in November 1939. This bridge at Thirteenth Street, still in use well into the twenty-first century, is also known as the "James U. Jackson Memorial Bridge."

After the bridge, Jackson continued building up the first six hundred acres of the town, until increased population and settlement convinced him to request a town charter. The state agreed, issued the charter, and the town (later city) of North Augusta, South Carolina, was officially incorporated on April 11, 1906.[89]

Herein lies a significant difference between James U. Jackson and Henry Shultz. Although both men named their towns after the cities of their birth, Shultz not only chose the name Hamburg but also built his town in competition, and likely revenge, against Augusta, Georgia. (See chapter 7.) In contrast, Jackson named his town North Augusta to honor Augusta, the city he loved, as well as where he was born.

Meanwhile, as the floods continued, so did the now desperate deliberation to find ways to prevent, or at least minimize, the destruction they caused. For the next few decades, whatever those decisions turned out to be would have a profound effect on the future of Hamburg.

Ever since the flood of 1888—which, in addition to destroying the Shultz Bridge did extensive damage to Augusta—the idea of building a levee along the river to protect the city had been proposed. Experts were consulted, and serious studies made; but nearly always, objections ruled the day. The cost, in excess of a million dollars, was prohibitive; an alternate suggestion to build a series of dams along the upper part of the river was preferred by some; and a cautious few dared to mention that a levee on the Augusta side might protect the city but annihilate Hamburg on the other.[90] Time would tell whether the latter objection was prophetic or just another reason not to proceed with the levee.

Then came the flood of 1908, with its severe damage to both sides of the river. In Augusta, even portions of the canal banks had to be rebuilt, and in Hamburg, many residents were forced to leave their destroyed homes along the river and move higher to Shultz Hill. After this, it didn't take long for Augustans to come to an obvious conclusion. Any method to counteract such destruction was now deemed more important than cost, and the city took another look at building that levee.

But progress was slow. There were so many details—selecting plans and builders, acquiring rights of way, obtaining that necessary though still objectionable funding, and satisfying a few wishful thinkers who wondered why they should take on such an exorbitant project when even these measures might not solve the river problem.

The 1912 flood changed more minds. The process continued, and the long, arduous task of building the levee was finally completed in time to "pass the test of another flood in December, 1919, with flying colors." Mayor James Littleton was then heard to say, "Our city is now safe from flood waters of the Savannah River."[91] Or maybe not.

Scarcely a decade later, neither "our city" nor its proud new levee were any match for three successive and increasingly devastating floods, one in 1928 and two more in 1929. This time even the Fifth Street Bridge, though damaged and repaired after the 1908 flood, was completely washed away when the final floodwaters rose higher than the top of the structure itself. Still, some portions of the levee did hold together so that, despite heavy damage, Augusta could be restored; and with time and federal assistance, the levee was strengthened and made more durable than it was before. Also, by 1931, the much more durable steel-girder-and-concrete Jefferson Davis Memorial Bridge at Fifth Street was ready for use.

Such was not the case with Hamburg. True to earlier warnings, the water even partially held back by the damaged levee on the Augusta side had nowhere else to go except across the river. Gradually, first in the lesser flood of 1928 and finally in the monstrous second flood of 1929, the town proper was almost completely washed away, and—there's no other way to say it—Hamburg was no more.

But what happened to the people of Hamburg? If there was any solace to this tragedy, it had to be in the timing. Both the rainfall and rising water, though constant, took nearly two weeks to reach their record-breaking highs. Thus, as far as we know, the residents had time to escape without any loss of life. Still, their homes were gone, and they needed new places to live. Some may have had family or other options away from Hamburg for at least temporary assistance. Fortunately for those who had no such connection, they wouldn't have any farther to go than atop those scenic hills Jackson had seen, or to what was still known as Shultz Hill. Thanks to both the American Red Cross and a local philanthropist, systems were soon in place for yet another new start for the remaining residents of Hamburg, even if the name of the town would not survive.

Of course, Shultz Hill and much of the surrounding area had been part of Hamburg all along and were still home to residents who moved uphill following the 1908 flood. But as North Augusta grew, more and more of the Shultz town was taken over by the new city, including at least the upper levels of Hamburg. Still, as generally happens whenever one area wanes or is claimed by another, the former name is usually retained until the local folks either pass away or become accustomed to the new name. At the same time, locally recognized communities are often formed within a larger municipality, even if, as in today's America, they don't have their own zip codes. All this should help explain the name changes in the former Hamburg area, which is now technically part of North Augusta but which, even today, may be called something else.

Before we move on to those new communities, however, we do need to remember what era we are talking about. Although many of the former slaves who populated Hamburg following emancipation did leave town after the massacre, the early twentieth century was still greatly influenced by segregation. Thus, as North Augusta grew, both in area and population, most Black residents continued to live in that part of the city formerly recognized as a predominantly Black town.

William Carpenter, the youngest child and only son of former slaves, was born in Hamburg in 1873. The Carpenter family remained in or near the town following the postmassacre exodus, a decision Carpenter's mother repeated when his father died in 1880. Possibly, becoming fatherless at such a young age and assuming a caretaker role for his mother and sisters prepared the adult William for both a prosperous life for himself and a desire to share that success with others.

Although he already owned a farm near Hamburg, his assets soon included the first Black-owned grocery store in Augusta, plus additional stores, before moving on to financial services and, eventually, more real estate. His equally remarkable philanthropy, though likely beginning much earlier, was well-known after 1922, when he purchased several tracts of land near Shultz Hill in Hamburg. This area, which then became known as Carpentersville, was not intended for his own use but would be offered without cost to any Hamburg resident needing a new home site following those devastating Savannah River floods.

Charles W. Carr may not have been a philanthropist in his own right, but as a disaster relief representative from the American Red Cross, he was among the first to arrive with a helping hand following the 1929 flood. After assessing the situation, Carr recommended that aid be given to renters and owners alike, as long as they agreed not to try resettling in Hamburg's flood-prone area. With total agreement to such an obvious stipulation, the residents were given financial and advisory help for everything from replacing household goods to securing lots and new or rebuilt homes. Many of those lots would be "secured" from William Carpenter.

Charles Carr seems to have taken a personal as well as professional interest in aiding Hamburg's flood victims—so much so that one of the streets running through the resettlement area was named Red Cross Street (now Boylan), and the larger part of the new community was called Carrsville after him. Later, perhaps to prevent confusion or because of the similarity between the names Carr and Carpenter, most of the area was then, as it still is today, known as Carrsville.

At this point we may have reached the official end of the town of Hamburg, but by no means are we at the end of the town's memory or effect. In many ways, as with our own ancestry, Hamburg's past is still with us. In our final chapter, we'll combine other significant facts about the area's more recent history with what is being done today to perpetuate, and perhaps to correct, the Hamburg legacy.

CHAPTER 41

Hamburg's Lasting Legacy

Although the once vibrant town has been missing for nearly a century, the subject of Hamburg, South Carolina, has been in the news a lot in recent years, and so have the questions. Besides wondering where the town was or why it isn't there anymore, except for those of us involved in the writing and research, most people just want to know "What's all this talk about Hamburg?"

Between the Bridges: The present shoreline of North
Augusta, South Carolina, formerly Market Street
in the town of Hamburg, South Carolina.
(Photo credit: Bruce Wilson)

Location? Approximately speaking, it is "Between the bridges." Put another way, standing near the Thirteenth Street Bridge over the Savannah River and looking downriver a short distance beyond the companion bridge at Fifth Street, we can get a good idea of the site and size of the town. Pausing to admire the magnificent new homes along Shoreline Drive today, we might even imagine a pair of buggy drivers clashing with a local militia there on what used to be called Market Street, the main thoroughfare on the edge of town.

Turning our eyes upward, past those homes and hills, we might also imagine another magnificent home, this one belonging to Henry Shultz, the founder of Hamburg, and the reason that area above the bluff is still known as Shultz Hill. Years later this site was home to the Hill Top Drive-In Theater, a new and short-lived entertainment venue that operated from 1951 into the 1970s. Since 1987, the same historic location, now listed as 802 East Martintown Road, has been home to the North Augusta Business Technology Center.

But after learning how Hamburg was destroyed, we realize something must have been done to tame the river, stop the flooding, and make the riverfront safe not only for new homes but also for the prestigious River Club Golf Course and, as announced in 2012, an exciting commercial venture planned for the other side of the Thirteenth Street bridge, known as "Project Jackson." As anticipated, before the end of the decade, this part of downtown North Augusta came alive with shops, restaurants, hotels, apartments, and, at the center of it all, the popular SRP Stadium, the new home of the Augusta Green Jackets baseball team. Some have even suggested that the renamed "Riverside Village," could be changed again to "New Hamburg."[92]

Yes, it didn't take long after that succession of early-twentieth-century floods to convince decision makers from the neighboring states and the federal government that something more reliable than canals and earthen levees must be found to control the too often out-of-control river.

About the only remedy mentioned so far but still untried was that "series of dams along the upper part of the river," an idea likely cast aside at the time because even the expensive levee didn't cost that much.[93] The dams would also take longer—fifty years, in fact, from the time this ultimate solution to the Savannah River problem was considered until the last of three upriver dams was completed at Lake Russell in 1984.

Coincidentally, in the late 1930s, or about the time the Georgia Power Company needed a new source of hydroelectric power to better serve the public and enable more industry, the US Army Corps of Engineers started surveying an area of the river above Augusta for a possible combination power plant and flood-control dam. After a federal commission recommended this very plan, President Franklin Roosevelt signed the bill authorizing construction of the Clarks Hill Dam and Power Plant on December 23, 1944.[94] Four years later, the corps and two thousand workers began the eight-year project, and the first dam to harness the flood-prone Savannah River was completed in 1956. (The second and northernmost dam would be in operation at Lake Hartwell by 1963.)

In addition to all its other benefits, the seventy-one-thousand-acre Clarks Hill Lake created by the dam was the corps' largest inland water project east of the Mississippi River to date, and likely the largest and most diverse recreation area ever created for the residents of Augusta, North Augusta, and surrounding villages and towns.

About the lake's name, we need to add one further note. Although both the lake and dam were named for the neighboring community of Clarks Hill, South Carolina, the name was officially changed in

1987 to Thurmond Lake and Dam, in honor of that state's senator, J. Strom Thurmond. Not everyone was happy with the name change, however—especially in Georgia, which is why Georgia lawmakers enacted legislation to keep the name "Clarks Hill Lake" on all their state's maps and signs. Now and then you can still hear a seasoned South Carolinian using the original name too. After all, the town of Clarks Hill is still on their side of the river.

Although much of our "last days" attention has been spent recounting the long but, thankfully, successful solution to the once destructive Savannah River, enough other stories about people, events, industry, and tangible remains emanating from that hilltop section of the town they still called Hamburg could be told to fill another book. Though we won't go that far, this book would not be complete without mentioning some of the more memorable and, in some cases, current topics associated with that place during that period of time.

Construction of the Clarks Hill Lake and Dam was by no means the only major building project occurring in the Central Savannah River Area (CSRA) during the mid-twentieth century. Of particular note, in June 1951, the E. I. DuPont Company and eight thousand workers arrived on the South Carolina side to begin building the Savannah River Plant (SRP; now called "Savannah River Site," or "SRS"), one of the largest nuclear weapons facilities in the country. A few years later, when the five reactors and dozens of related facilities were completed, the construction crew was replaced by more than eleven thousand engineers, plant operators, and other personnel who came there to stay.

Meanwhile, southwest of Augusta on the Georgia side, the former World War II Army training center, then called Camp Gordon, increased in size and personnel for other military purposes until 1956, when the name of the installation was changed to Fort Gordon and the facility became the home of the US Army Signal Corps.

Population explosion, anyone? As a result of SRP alone, the area experienced an increase of forty-six thousand new residents. Thus, in addition to the major construction sites, imagine the number of homes, buildings and building supplies needed to house and support that many people. That must have been good news for one particular upper Hamburg industry—the more than half a dozen brick factories located there.

Really? That many suppliers of the same product in just one town? Other than the voluminous need, the South Carolina side of the river appears to have achieved another coup. Besides their cotton honors of years before (see chapter 13), the clay for their bricks was also known to be superior to that found across the river, which meant Georgia builders preferred South Carolina bricks too. One outstanding Augusta example of that superior choice is the Sacred Heart Catholic Church (now Cultural Center) on Greene Street, which is still in good condition and in use though built between 1898 and 1900, more than a century ago.

But you know what people say about all work and no play. With all those engineers, soldiers, and construction workers around, Hamburg was quick to respond. Restaurants, nightclubs, pool halls, and more launched the town's newest industry—a mixture of recreation and entertainment. At least two of those establishments have surviving reputations, including Palmetto Park and Pond on the east side of town, where folks could swim during the day and go dancing in the nighttime. This locale must have had a widespread reputation at the time, for it was known to attract such famous entertainers as Louis Armstrong and Ella Fitzgerald.

The other, a nightclub known as the Club Royal, located just west of the Fifth Street Bridge, even played a part in a major motion picture. Renowned actress Joanne Woodward, who also had local roots, earned an Oscar for her starring role in *The Three Faces of Eve*, the story of a North Augusta woman suffering from multiple personality disorder, based on the best-selling book by the two Augusta psychiatrists, Drs. Corbett H. Thigpen and Hervey M. Cleckley, who treated her. The woman, Christine Costner Sizemore, confirmed that the Club Royal was indeed where her "party personality," Eve Black, sang and danced for local soldiers and other patrons before she returned home as the demure but unhappy Eve White. Fortunately, filming was completed before the nightclub burned to the ground, which occurred scarcely a month before the movie premiered at Augusta's Miller Theater on September 18, 1957.[95]

Fortunately again, some of the original Hamburg buildings did survive their flood destruction well enough to be dismantled and, along with the town's remaining people, moved to that upper section of the old Hamburg. In addition to a few salvageable homes, at least three public structures in use or in various stages of recovery today still stand in the Carrsville section of North Augusta or nearby, partly answering that question asked at the beginning of the chapter: "What's all this talk about Hamburg?"

There has been plenty of talk—and action—about the first of those structures. Providence Baptist Church, the completely restored and renamed First Providence Baptist Church on Barton Road today, was founded in Hamburg in 1860 as a mission of Augusta's Thankful Baptist Church. Before then there was no church in town for Blacks to attend, and traveling to the Augusta church was difficult or just too far.

But after the destruction of 1929, members of the church, along with help from Thankful Baptist and other area churches, took apart the wooden building, combined reusable remnants with other salvaged materials, and rebuilt the church on one of those lots provided by William Carpenter in 1932. Sometime later, both a brick exterior and education annex were added to the building. Following completion of a larger and more modern sanctuary next door in 1992, the original structure became the Alexander Pope Resource Center, bearing the name of the church's current and longtime pastor, while the annex is now a popular preschool and daycare center.

Providence Baptist Church.
(Photo credit: Bruce Wilson)

As if all this weren't legacy enough, two other churches, formed out of the original Providence Baptist and established in that upper Hamburg area even before the relocation of First Providence, are still thriving North Augusta congregations today. Second Providence Baptist, with beginnings as early as 1899, is located at 1202 Old Edgefield Road, while Carpentersville Baptist remains at 415 Carpentersville Road, where it was established in 1925.

Across the street from First Providence stands Hamburg's Society Building, the second structure to be reclaimed, piece by piece, from the flood-destroyed town and reassembled in its present location, also in 1932. Unlike Providence Baptist, however, which has always been a church, this building has had a multipurpose history. Besides serving first as home to the Young Men's Union Association, later as a school for Black children during segregation, and, after 1988, as the location of North Augusta's Simmons Lodge No. 571, other groups have also made use of this large open space for a variety of meetings or events.

But the Society Building's wooden exterior was never overlaid with brick like its neighbor across the street. Thus, in time, the weathered clapboards took on that ugly gray-black appearance of a structure waiting for demolition.

"Not if we have anything to say about it!" declared about as many groups as ever occupied the building during its decades of service to the community. For a number of years now, these historians, civic organizations, preservation groups, and local businesses have been pooling their time, interest, and resources in a major effort to save yet another part of the reviving Hamburg story.

Like the building itself, from restoration to plans for the future, this project is also multipurpose and ongoing. Yet even before a meeting, an occupant, or a suggested museum materializes inside, several projects or events have already occurred around or on the grounds outside. One highly celebrated event took place Sunday afternoon, March 6, 2016, on the front lawn, when both a standing

Hamburg Massacre marker and, on the ground below, a memorial stone etched with the names of all eight men killed on that day were unveiled.

Society Building in background, Hamburg
Massacre marker and memorial stone in front.
(Photo credit: Bruce Wilson)

Eight men? Yes, not just the one White man, and not just the seven Black men, but all eight together, in alphabetical order: Allen Attaway, Jim Cook, Thomas Meriwether, Albert Myniart, Nelder Parker, Moses Parks, David Phillips, and Hampton Stephens. Eight men were honored on this carefully chosen date, almost one hundred years to the day after, in a far different ceremony across town, the

Meriwether Monument was unveiled in 1916. (See chapter 39.) This day, with its overtones of the biblical message "overcoming evil with good" (Romans 12:21), was a powerful experience for the overflow crowd, who gathered in the old Providence Baptist Church sanctuary to reflect on the meaning of what they had just witnessed.

Along with North Augusta Heritage Council president Milledge Murray, Aiken County Historical Museum executive director Brenda Baratto, then North Augusta mayor Lark Jones, and master of ceremonies Wayne O'Bryant, two guests familiar with the Hamburg story also shared their thoughts on the day's significance.

"The only way to understand history is to know what *did* happen," said Stephen Budiansky, author of the 2008 book *The Bloody Shirt: Terror After Appomattox.* In his research on Hamburg and four other Reconstruction-era sites of racial and political violence, this author had taken his own advice, visited the area, and, with the aid and expertise of local historian Peter Hughes, written a lengthy account of Hamburg's history, with special attention to the massacre. The reason for Budiansky's presence on what is still called Hamburg Marker Day was to celebrate and commend those who had carried this historic update from talk to action.

Continuing along the same theme, Georgia Southern University professor Dr. Jonathan Bryant then spoke of his and other educators' efforts to make sure their students know the truth about that important but little understood period called Reconstruction. Professor Bryant particularly wanted his African American students to learn not just hearsay or "manipulated memory" but what "did happen" to their ancestors during that troubled time.

This day was certainly a morale boost for those who had worked so diligently not only to initiate the renovation of the Society Building but also to renovate the *record* of that long-ago, tragic

Hamburg day. As the concurring editor of the *North Augusta Star* had expressed some months before, "The Hamburg Massacre isn't a part of history that needs to be buried, no matter how ugly a piece of history it is."[96]

As commendable as all this research had been, there still was a dilapidated building that would never become a museum in its current condition. But the excitement generated by those efforts and this day was catching. Before long, led by the North Augusta Heritage Council and members of the newly formed Historic North Augusta organization, an outpouring of donors, suppliers, and skilled workers began offering their resources, time, and labor to see this project through. As of this writing, four years after Marker Day, another sign has been placed in front of the building with a list of principal sponsors who have contributed to this effort so far.

Realizing that the building's first occupant, the Young Men's Union Association, had been formed to ensure that everyone in Hamburg could have a proper burial, the Rowland-Ford Funeral Home was eager to assist in funding the costly renovation. Other donations have also been received from North Augusta's Optimist and Sertoma Clubs, and from many interested individuals.

Among the first to respond to the actual renovation was Brighter Side Roofing, the company who, with donated labor, has completed the lengthy task of replacing the building's roof. Other sponsors—those who have replaced windows and doors, reinforced the foundation, begun refurbishing the exterior, or donated myriad supplies needed for the entire renovation—include US Lumber Company, Maner Builders Supply, Reliable Equipment Rental, and Lowe's.

Although more work needs to be done on the outside as well as the interior, the new Hamburg Museum could well become a reality in the near future. And if that day comes, likely no one will be happier than Marker Day master of ceremonies Wayne O'Bryant, who also is a Hamburg descendant.

"Sunday's gathering was not just about a memorial and a dedication, but also about a vision," O'Bryant told reporter James Folker for a front-page story in the *Augusta Chronicle* the following day.[97] After spending years researching and documenting both his family background and that of the town, O'Bryant is often called a Hamburg expert, and he doesn't plan to stop with just a museum. Thinking not only of his own heritage, he believes the area around the Society Building could be developed into a park or perhaps a Hamburg district, where other African Americans can learn about their heritage. This project would likely be in partnership with neighboring First Providence, since a number of well-known Hamburg residents, including Prince Rivers, were once active members of the original church.

We leave discussion of the Society Building for now to acknowledge not a group or an organization this time, but the individual who restored the old Hamburg depot, that third resurrected building once located in the ruined town of Hamburg.

Mr. Gordon Farmer, a World War II veteran who, with his brother, Pierce, founded the Augusta Concrete Block Company in North Augusta, wasn't the first to attempt such a rescue. But this man, who in his spare time was also a history buff and collector of antiques, couldn't help noticing the little depot sitting in disrepair on Southern Railroad property nearby. Fearing it could be slated for demolition, he asked whether he might purchase the building and have it restored. No, the railroad folks said, he wouldn't need to purchase the building, but if he would move it to his property for that purpose, they would give it to him. Thus, both the giver and receiver were happy when Farmer moved the small building to his concrete plant—which incidentally was located on several acres of the former upper Hamburg site—where it was restored and still stands.

Old Hamburg depot.
(Photo credit: Bruce Wilson)

The little building, about the size of a two-car garage, with double doors, a narrow front porch, and relics inside, is likely not the original Charleston-Hamburg Railroad depot placed on land donated by Henry Shultz in the 1830s (see chapter 17), but a replacement built some time later, when the railroad company itself changed hands. Still, with its Hamburg origin, and current home on actual Hamburg land, the Farmer family certainly have a historic gem on their hands and property. Organizers of the Aiken County Centennial in 1971 must have thought so after the once condemned depot was restored and on display for the gala occasion.

As Farmer's wife, Martha Claire, recalls, along with the depot on that special celebration day, someone brought a replica of another

Hamburg Railroad antique, the *Best Friend*, the first steam engine to run on the historic Charleston and Hamburg Railroad in 1833. The stand-in for that "little engine that could" was pulled manually along an old set of railroad tracks still located on the Augusta Concrete Block Company grounds, which were, appropriately, right beside the depot.

Now, with the church and depot fully restored and the Society Building renovation well underway, we change scenes again to find out what is being done with that controversial Hamburg monument across town. Although structural restoration is not the concern this time, likely more time, discussion, and activity have been spent just deciding what should be done with the Meriwether Monument than on all the other updates so far.

Still, as difficult as this decision has been, in another significant change to the Hamburg story from a century ago, both of these remaining projects, the Society Building and the Meriwether Monument, have been moving hand-in-hand with many of the same movers all along—the same movers, that is, plus a number of newcomers to the monument table. In addition to the aforementioned North Augusta Heritage Council, Historic North Augusta, and the Aiken County Historical Museum, ever since their Hamburg Exhibit in 2012, the Arts and Heritage Center of North Augusta, located in the city's Municipal Building, has been on board with this issue too.

But talk about the monument has reached far beyond historic organizations. Besides growing public interest—likely sparked by the current obsession with historic monuments in general—because this one sits on public land and the city council is the proper body responsible for what happens there, they are ultimately the ones who will make the final decision regarding retention, alteration, or removal of the Meriwether Monument. And they, along with the current mayor, Robert Pettit, have met this challenge head-on.

As the administrators would soon learn and encourage, that monument in the center of town was fast becoming the center of attention for just about everyone they met or heard from via phone, email, regular mail or, indirectly, through reports in area newspapers or on radio and TV. As they would also learn, unlike those who are trying to shape this decision along historic or aesthetic grounds, that mountain of public opinion stretches anywhere from those who adamantly believe "this atrocity should be torn down" to those who, just as emphatically, oppose "defacing, destroying, or removing any historic monuments" in their city of North Augusta, South Carolina.

Two others, though not in favor of the monument, have offered specific suggestions for reducing its offensive presence. Freelance journalist Kenton J. Makin first called on the council to take the monument down "or at the very least ... to make a formal denouncement of the monument, what it stands for, and what it reads."[98] Also, in an article for the August 23, 2017, edition of the *North Augusta Star*, journalist Phyllis Britt expressed her opposition like this: "I don't advocate destroying statues. They are a part of our history that cannot be denied. But they don't belong in the center of town ... where their presence is a constant reminder of a time in our history that should not instill pride."[99] Instead, she advocated placing them in a museum where relevant items are dedicated to a certain time and place in our history.

Still, before any suggestion could be considered or any decision made regarding the monument, one further opinion had to be known. As the mayor and council knew, according to the South Carolina Heritage Act, Section 10-1-165, (1) "No Revolutionary War, War of 1812, War Between the States (or any other war) monuments or memorials erected on public property of the State ... may be relocated, removed, disturbed, or altered," and (2) "the provisions of this section may only be amended or repealed upon passage of an act which has received a two-thirds vote on the third reading of the bill in each branch of the General Assembly."

But this monument wasn't really a war memorial, was it? McKie Meriwether died as a result of a local incident that happened a full decade after the war ended. Still, because the monument was erected on public land, Mayor Pettit asked city attorney Kelly Zier to contact the South Carolina Attorney General's office for their opinion as to whether or not the Meriwether Monument is covered by the act. Although inconclusive, Solicitor General Robert Cook offered the following explanation in his September 28, 2017, reply: "As we discussed by phone, litigation is pending challenging the validity of the Heritage Act ... Because of this, it would be inappropriate to comment on your request at this time." However, Solicitor Cook did indicate their office believed in both the validity of the act and that, where historic monuments are concerned, the act may be amended to include more than monuments of war.

Choosing urgency over patience, Mayor Pettit and the council decided not to wait for litigation to end. Instead, following further study, sessions with interested groups and individuals, and the possibility that the Heritage Act may indeed prevent removal or alteration of the monument, a consensus appears to be taking shape on how to resolve this heated debate among those on both the retention and removal sides of the monument issue.

As the discussion continues, this new development takes into consideration the retention side's concern that, to remove the monument is to destroy history. Furthermore, if this monument comes down, what's to prevent removal of the next monument, or the changing of the name of a street, building, community, or so on, just because the person being honored in one of these ways offends someone?

At the same time, even if removing the monument proves to be against the law, those advocating some form of change wonder how the monument might become an asset rather than a liability to the community. Why not augment that history, they ask, by adding markers or symbols near the monument to explain the circumstances of that time and contrast them with the prevailing thought and culture of today? The Meriwether Monument could then become an educational tool, whereas removal would be to lose an opportunity to teach valuable lessons from that history.

Continuing this line of thinking, in conjunction with the city council, historians, public opinion, and his own personal study, after a full year of attention to the monument, in November 2018, Mayor Pettit released his extensive report to the council detailing what he had learned from a variety of sources and offering these conclusions and recommendations for what should be done with the monument:

> __Removing or altering the monument is not a viable option;
>
> __Leaving Calhoun Park unchanged is not an option;
>
> __Calhoun Park can be made a positive, educational experience; and
>
> __A defined, distinct area, surrounding the monument should be created providing educational opportunities for visitors as a counterpoint to the viewpoints expressed by the text on the monument.[100]

It didn't take long for the council, an appointed committee, and others concerned with the monument resolution to agree with the mayor's recommendations or to begin the process of deciding just how that enhanced educational area near the monument will be implemented.

These and other suggestions are still in the planning and decision stage. But with funding for the project in the mayor's 2020 budget, interested parties are hopeful that the updated and newly purposed Meriwether Monument section of Calhoun Park will be ready for viewing sooner rather than later.

In addition to restoring Hamburg's physical legacy, other projects designed to tell the Hamburg story are either in the planning stage or nearing completion. For the reader, longtime resident and former Heritage Council president, Milledge Murray, whose personal Hamburg ancestry goes back to the days of Henry Shultz, has spearheaded a companion book to this volume compiled by the Heritage Committee of the Arts and Heritage Center of North Augusta. For the viewer, other plans are being developed. Hardly anyone has worked longer to revive Hamburg's latter history than the now former executive director of the Aiken County Historical Museum Brenda Baratto. As news of her research spread across the state, she began receiving calls about the former town from a number of interested South Carolina schools. After learning about a new online tool for spreading just such information, called "A Virtual Tour," she set a plan in motion to educate those inquiring schools about Hamburg.

It would be a long process and would include many parts and players. The proposed project combines interviews with regional historians; copies of historic photos, newspaper clippings, and other documents; plus an actual walk through a now overgrown section of the former town. This Hamburg tour has finally progressed from filming to editing. Although Brenda retired from the museum in 2018, her successor, Lauren Virgo, has continued to oversee the project and expects it will be available for viewing sometime within the 2020–2021 school year.

Though not as far into the planning stage as the virtual tour, that initial idea to turn the Society Building into a museum or turn the surrounding area into a Hamburg district may soon be underway. According to spokesman Wayne O'Bryant, together with Pastor Alexander Pope Jr. and members of First Providence Baptist Church, signs and murals depicting a number of former African American–owned stores and other businesses may soon line Barton Road from the Society Building to the still standing studio at the corner of Buena Vista Avenue, where the well-known soul singer James Brown once recorded many of his popular music albums.

And by all means, in conjunction with Simmons Lodge, who still own the Society Building but will confine their operation to the upper level after renovation is complete, that much desired Hamburg Museum is still planned for the ground floor. Mr. O'Bryant's enthusiasm, along with that of First Providence and assistance from the North Augusta government, will see to that.

In summary, following a near century of obscurity, whether through the reading of a book, the visiting of a museum, the viewing of a virtual tour, or the welcoming of busloads of schoolchildren and tourists to Barton Road and the updated Calhoun Park, Mayor Robert Pettit, the North Augusta City Council, Hamburg descendants Wayne O'Bryant and Milledge Murray, and all who have had a part in updating the Hamburg memory, hope their efforts will offer not just a good story but also a new sense of political, racial, and communal unity to all our hometowns and historic places.

But lest we forget, although we have spent nearly half our time on just one major event and its aftermath, the town of Hamburg, South Carolina, did not begin in 1876; nor did it end with a raging flood in

1929. Fifty years of significant interest and achievement occurred in the town prior to the massacre, and at least two visible reminders in the area today should help extend the entire Hamburg legacy far into the future. In keeping with our title and overall theme, one of those reminders is another monument.

Berry Benson was born in Hamburg in 1843 and, at the age of seventeen, became a Confederate soldier at the start of the Civil War. After an exemplary record, plus his wounds, imprisonment, escape, and service to the end of the war, Sgt. Benson enjoyed the title of "war hero" for the rest of his life. Following a brief stint in Texas as a cotton broker, he and his family settled in Augusta, where he spent his postwar years working as an accountant and dedicating himself to worthy causes, especially those in any way connected to the people and events of the war. Thus, it was no surprise when Benson himself became an important part of one of those worthy causes.

In 1868, the Ladies Memorial Association of Augusta was formed for the purpose of caring for the graves of Confederate dead, with the ultimate goal of erecting a monument in their honor. Although that goal would take ten years, by 1875, plans were sufficiently in place to begin assembling the tallest and, some say, the most admired Confederate war monument in the state of Georgia.

Located in the median of the 700 block of Broad Street in Augusta, the seventy-six-foot obelisk, with its Georgia granite base topped by a tapering Italian-marble shaft, was designed by ornamental architects Van Gunden and Young of Philadelphia, and built by the Theodore Markwalter firm of Augusta. Most striking are the five life-sized marble statues carved to resemble figures in photographs sent to sculptor Antonio Fontana in Carrara, Italy, for that purpose. Four of the statues, each standing on a corner of the granite base, are of Confederate generals: Robert E. Lee, who represented the

Confederacy; Thomas "Stonewall" Jackson, of Virginia; Thomas R. R. Cobb, of the state of Georgia; and William H. T. Walker, from Augusta.

Confederate monument in Augusta.
(Photo credit: Milledge Murray)

And the fifth statue? Standing at the very top, and leaning on the rifle he famously did not surrender at Appomattox, is the likeness of one Berry Benson, originally from Hamburg, South Carolina, but symbolizing enlisted men from every state in the Confederacy who were lost in the recent war.

By noon on October 31, 1878, an estimated ten thousand people, including sixteen carriages carrying dignitaries, crowded into Broad Street to dedicate the monument. Among the honored guests were Georgia governor Alfred Colquitt; General "Stonewall" Jackson's widow, Mary Anna; Georgia historian Charles C. Jones, who gave the dedicatory speech; and, somewhere in the crowd, incognito on the ground (as he is deemed to be at the top of the statue), one former enlisted soldier known by the locals as Berry Benson.[101]

The other visible reminder of the town has already been mentioned in this chapter, yet perhaps not with that lingering legacy connection in mind. Now, thinking back two centuries to a man gazing at a cornfield across the river from Augusta, it is clear that there never would have been a Hamburg without the vision—and temperament—of Henry Shultz. The bustling, successful trading center he hoped would rival the Georgia city became a reality for a while, until circumstances, along with the unruly Savannah River, took his town down.

But if that same man were to gaze across the river today and see not a cornfield, not even the eventual destruction of his once flourishing town, but a thriving city, he might also remember a railroad steam engine, the *Phoenix*, which was assembled from the remnants of the ruined *Best Friend of Charleston*, that first steam engine to run on the historic Charleston and Hamburg Railroad in 1833. (See chapter 20.)

As we already know, the name of the *Phoenix* is based on a bird of Greek myth that rose to life from the ashes of its predecessor. Though not a myth, but in similar fashion, this new city rising prominently from the banks of the now tamed Savannah River may be called North Augusta, but we can imagine our man Shultz standing there in admiration and recollection of that other town he once crossed an ocean and a river to give birth.

The name Henry Shultz, as well as that of his town, will be forever linked in the lasting legacy of Hamburg, South Carolina.

AFTERWORD

If you have reached this page after reading from the beginning, you already know the main purpose of this book was to present the Hamburg story in as complete and factual a manner as possible, according to the information we had at the time. You also may remember some discussion about the word "history" or how and why our "facts" don't always agree with those of someone else. As of this date, near the end of 2020, because of recent developments throughout the country, including the vicinity of the former town of Hamburg, this history book needs some added clarification.

The year 2020 was eventful. On the heels of the novel coronavirus pandemic, which started early and continues to bring illness, even death, to many of our citizens, by late spring a pandemic of another kind swept in to further complicate our lives. Ironically, that second assault bears a strong resemblance to the late 1800s, or the very time frame when the latter part of the Hamburg story took place.

A series of White-on-Black killings, often by law enforcement officers trying to arrest resisting offenders, quickly sparked racial controversy wherever they occurred. Like the virus, this controversy also spread quickly, first in area, and then in topic. Because 2020, like 1876, was an election year, politics soon joined race as a reason to fuel the growing national divide.

Sleeping giants were awakened as throngs of activists revisited the entire scope of slavery and racial injustice, and congregated around any post–Civil War symbol of that era still in existence. Hardly a day goes by that we don't hear of another statue or monument toppled or threatened with destruction. Although both monuments addressed prominently in this book have been targeted for removal, unlike the violence that has occurred elsewhere, most local protests have been law-abiding and peaceful. Those protesting the Meriwether Monument have even begun a campaign to seek a change to the South Carolina Heritage Act addressed by the state attorney general, which may be made if two-thirds of the legislators vote to do so. (See chapter 41.) Also, across the river, thus far there has been only the suggestion to move the Confederate monument from the center of town to a nearby cemetery where many Confederate war dead are buried.

At this point, however, no one knows what, if anything, will happen to these two monuments. Perhaps the plan to turn Calhoun Park into an educational destination, with or without the Meriwether Monument, will still take place. But this afterword has been added to inform the reader that the end of chapter 41 may not be the final word on the Hamburg Legacy after all. Whatever happens, I would just like to compliment both the ones who still want to take the monument down, for their peaceful and legal efforts to achieve their goal, and the North Augusta City Council and others who still have the plan in place to make the Meriwether Monument in Calhoun Park an asset rather than a liability.

Barbara Seaborn, January 2021

SOURCES

Britt, Phyllis. "It's Time to Put Racial Animosity Aside." *North Augusta Star*, August 23, 2017.

Budiansky, Stephen. *The Bloody Shirt: Terror After Appomattox*. New York: Viking Penguin, 2008.

Cashin, Edward J., Jr. *The Brightest Arm of the Savannah: The Augusta Canal, 1845–2000*. Augusta, GA: Augusta Canal Authority, 2002.

_____. *The Story of Augusta*. Spartanburg, SC: The Reprint Company, 1991.

Chapman, John A. *History of Edgefield County, South Carolina*. Greenville, SC: Southern Historical Press, 2009.

Cordle, Charles G. "Henry Shultz and the Founding of Hamburg, South Carolina." In *Studies in Georgia History and Government*. Athens, GA: University of Georgia Press, 1940.

Fetters, Thomas. *The Charleston & Hamburg: A South Carolina Railroad and an American Legacy*. Charleston, SC: The History Press, 2008.

Folker, James. "Blacks Killed in 1876 Get Marker." *Augusta Chronicle*, March 7, 2016.

_____. "North Augusta Dealing with Monument Issue." *Augusta Chronicle*, September 27, 2017.

Foner, Eric. *Reconstruction: America's Unfinished Revolution, 1863–1877*. Francis Parkman Prize Edition. New York: History Book Club, by arrangement with Harper-Collins Publishers, 2005.

Heckel, Jenny. *Remembering Meriwether: White Carolinian Manipulation of the Memory of the Hamburg Massacre of 1876*.

A thesis presented to the Graduate School of Clemson University. Clemson, South Carolina, December 2016.

Hughes, Peter. "Images of the Augusta Bridge." January 4, 2017. https://henryshultz.wordpress.com/2017/01/04/images-of-the-augusta-bridge

————. "The Sixth Hamburg Mechanic's Festival." *Carolina Herald and Newsletter*, official publication of the South Carolina Genealogical Society, April, May, and June 2010.

Lawrence, Kay. "Hamburg—Empire Built on a Grudge." In *Heroes, Horses, & High Society: Aiken from 1540*. Reprint edition. Columbia, SC: R. L. Bryan Company, 1989.

The Learning Network. "March 2, 1877: Hayes Declared Winner in Disputed Presidential Election." *New York Times*, March 2, 2012.

Love, Edith Bell. "Henry Shultz's Spite Town." *Sandlapper*, May 1968.

Miscellaneous Document of the US Senate, Forty-Fourth Congress, Second Session. Selected Testimony from: "Denial of the Elective Franchise in South Carolina at the Elections of 1875 and 1876, December 5, 1876. Washington: Government Printing Office, 1877."

Morse, Joseph Laffan. "The Electoral Commission of 1877." In *Universal Standard Encyclopedia*. New York: Standard Reference Works, 1956–1957.

Nesbitt, Jim. "County, once booming, now shadows town it used to rival." *The Augusta Chronicle*, May 25, 2011.

Newman, Joseph. "200 Years, A Bicentennial Illustrated History of the United States." *US News & World Report,* 1973.

Pettit, Robert. *Report to the City Council of North Augusta: Recommendations Regarding the Meriwether Monument in Calhoun Park*, November 2018.

Rhodes, Don. "Exhibit celebrates heyday of Palmetto Park." *Augusta Chronicle.* February 14, 2010. https://www.augustachronicle. com/article/20100214/NEWS/302149925.

_____. "Real-Life Eve of 'Three Faces of Eve' honored at Funeral." *Augusta Chronicle.* August 3, 2016. www.augustachronicle.com.

_____. "The 1929 Flood That Spelled the End for Hamburg." Displayed on a wall plaque for the 2012 Hamburg Exhibit at the North Augusta Arts and Heritage Center, North Augusta, South Carolina.

Rosson, Elizabeth Murphy, ed. *History of North Augusta, South Carolina.* North Augusta, SC: The North Augusta Historical Society, 1980.

Rubin, Hyman S., III. "Election of 1876." *The South Carolina Encyclopedia.* Columbia: The University of South Carolina, 2016.

Seaborn, Barbara. *As Long as the Rivers Run: Highlights from Columbia County's Past.* Martinez, GA: Crown Point Publishing, 2011.

Stone, William. "In Regards to the Battle of Hamburg." Report submitted to Daniel H. Chamberlain, governor of South Carolina, July 12, 1876.

Taylor, Rosser. "Hamburg: An Experiment in Town Promotion." *North Carolina Historical Review* II, January 1934, pages 20–28.

Tillman, Benjamin Ryan. "The Struggles of 1876." Address delivered to the Red Shirt Reunion in Anderson, South Carolina. August 25, 1909.

Vandervelde, Isabel. *Aiken County, the Only South Carolina County Founded During Reconstruction.* Spartanburg, SC: The Reprint Company, 1999.

Voigt-Lassen, Irene. "Ein Dahmer wurde Stadtebauer an der Savannah." (A Citizen of Dahme Built a City on the Savannah.) Translated by Jurgen Moller. Contribution 36 in volume 9 of the annual proceedings for local history from Oldenburg in Holstein, Germany, 1965.

Woodworth, Steven E., and Kenneth J. Winkler, *Atlas of the Civil War*. New York: Oxford University Press, 2004.

ENDNOTES

[1] Irene Voigt-Lassen, "Ein Dahmer wurde Stadtebauer an der Savannah" (A Citizen of Dahme Built a City on the Savannah), trans. Jurgen Moller, in the annual proceedings for local history, Oldenburg in Holstein, Germany, contribution 36 in volume 9 (1965), 245–49.

[2] *Edgefield Advertiser*, April 29, 1846.

[3] Peter Hughes, "Images of the Augusta Bridge," January 4, 2017. https://henryshultz.wordpress.com/2017/01/04/images-of-the-augusta-bridge/.

[4] *Augusta Chronicle*, October 1, 1817.

[5] Elizabeth Murphy Rosson, ed. *History of North Augusta, South Carolina*, Volume 1, (North Augusta, SC: The North Augusta Historical Society, 1980), 12.

[6] Charles Cordle, "Henry Shultz and the Founding of Hamburg, South Carolina," in *Studies in Georgia History and Government* (Athens, GA: University of Georgia Press, 1940), 80.

[7] Edward J. Cashin, *The Story of Augusta* (Spartanburg, SC: The Reprint Company, 1991), 71.

[8] Cordle, "Henry Shultz," 80.

[9] Edith Bell Love, "Henry Shultz's Spite Town," *Sandlapper*, May 1968.

[10] Love, "Henry Schultz's."

[11] "McKinne's Mortgage Relative to the Bridge Case," *Hamburg Journal*, July 23, 1842.

[12] Hughes, "Images."

[13] "McKinne's Mortgage Relative to the Bridge Case," *Hamburg Journal*, July 23, 1842.

[14] Cordle, "Henry Schultz," 82.

[15] *Charleston Courier*, November 27, 1823.

[16] Cordle, "Henry Schultz," 83–84.

[17] Barbara Seaborn, *As Long as the Rivers Run: Highlights of Columbia County's Past* (Crown Point: Martinez, GA, 2011).

[18] Cordle, "Henry Schultz," 85.

[19] Cordle, 89.

[20] Cordle, 88.

21 *Augusta Chronicle & Georgia Advertiser*, July 3, 1824.

22 Hughes, "The Sixth Hamburg Mechanic's Festival," *Carolina Herald and Newsletter*, official publication of the South Carolina Genealogical Society, April, May, and June, 2010.

23 Hughes, "Sixth Hamburg Mechanic's Festival."

24 *Augusta Chronicle*, late 1827.

25 Seaborn, *As Long as the Rivers Run*, 180–81.

26 Thomas Fetters, *The Charleston & Hamburg: A South Carolina Railroad and an American Legacy* (Charleston, South Carolina: The History Press, 2008), 14.

27 Fetters, *"The Charleston & Hamburg,"* 15.

28 Fetters, 16.

29 Fetters, 22.

30 Fetters, 23–24.

31 Newspaper quotes and information compiled from the South Carolina Library in Columbia, South Carolina, for the 2012 Hamburg Exhibit by Peter Hughes.

32 Business information compiled for the 2012 Hamburg Exhibit by Don Rhodes.

33 Sources for the "Ladies of Hamburg" segment include *The South Carolina Encyclopedia*, *The National Women's History Museum*, and the *Augusta Chronicle*.

34 Rosser Taylor, "Hamburg: An Experiment in Town Promotion," *North Carolina Historical Review* II, January 1934, 24.

35 Taylor, "Hamburg," 32.

36 Love, "Henry Schultz's."

37 Taylor, "Hamburg," 32.

38 Augusta Canal information from Edward J. Cashin Jr., *The Brightest Arm of the Savannah: The Augusta Canal, 1845–2000* (Augusta, GA: Augusta Canal Authority, 2002); Seaborn, *As Long as the Rivers Run*.

39 Edgefield District Census records on file at the Old Edgefield Genealogical Library, housed in the Tompkins Library in Edgefield, South Carolina.

40 Rosson, *History of North Augusta*, 15.

41 Kay Lawrence, "Hamburg—Empire Built on a Grudge," in *Heroes, Horses, & High Society: Aiken from 1540*, reprint edition (Columbia, SC: R. L. Bryan Company, 1989), 75.

42 Love, "Henry Shultz's."

43 Woodworth and Winkle, eds., *Oxford Atlas of the Civil War* (New York: Oxford University Press, 2004), 290.

[44] Joseph Newman, "200 Years, A Bicentennial Illustrated History of the United States," *US News & World Report*, 1973, 56.

[45] Cashin, *Story*, 132.

[46] Eric Foner, *Reconstruction: America's Unfinished Revolution, 1863–1877*, Francis Parkman Prize edition (New York: History Book Club, by arrangement with Harper-Collins Publishers, Inc., 2005), 602.

[47] Foner, *Reconstruction*, ix.

[48] Foner, 354.

[49] Woodworth and Winkle, *Oxford Atlas*, 338–40.

[50] Stephen Budiansky, *The Bloody Shirt: Terror After Appomattox* (New York: Viking Penguin, 2008), 225.

[51] William Stone, "In Regards to the Battle of Hamburg," submitted to D. H. Chamberlain, governor of South Carolina, July 12, 1876.

[52] Isabel Vandervelde, *Aiken County: The Only South Carolina County Founded During Reconstruction* (Spartanburg, South Carolina: The Reprint Company, 1999), 195.

[53] Testimony of Dock Adams, "Denial of the Elective Franchise in South Carolina," December 5, 1876.

[54] Budiansky, *The Bloody Shirt*, 233–36.

[55] Budiansky, 239.

[56] Budiansky, 242.

[57] Stone, "In Regards to the Battle."

[58] Vandervelde, *Aiken County*, 421–44.

[59] Budiansky, *The Bloody Shirt*, 245.

[60] Vandervelde, *Aiken County*, 421–44.

[61] Budiansky, *The Bloody Shirt*, 239.

[62] Benjamin Tillman, "The Struggles of 1876," speech delivered at the Red Shirt Reunion, August 25, 1909.

[63] Tillman.

[64] Vandervelde, *Aiken County*, 416.

[65] Budiansky, *The Bloody Shirt*, 244.

[66] Tillman, "The Struggles of 1876."

[67] Vandervelde, *Aiken County*, 165–66.

[68] Budiansky, *The Bloody Shirt*, 246.

[69] Budiansky, 248.

[70] Budiansky, 248.

[71] Hyman S. Rubin III, "Election of 1876," *The South Carolina Encyclopedia* (Columbia: The University of South Carolina, 2016).

[72] Budiansky, *The Bloody Shirt*, 250.

[73] Budiansky, 250.

[74] Joseph Laffan Morse, "The Electoral Commission of 1877," in *Universal Standard Encyclopedia* (New York: Standard Reference Works 1956–1957).

[75] Budiansky, *The Bloody Shirt,* 250–51.

[76] Budiansky, 250–51.

[77] Budiansky, 252.

[78] Budiansky, 253.

[79] Budiansky, 253.

[80] Budiansky, 253.

[81] Vandervelde, *Aiken County*, 443.

[82] Jim Nesbitt, "County, once booming, now shadows town it used to rival," *Augusta Chronicle*, May 25, 2011.

[83] Jenny Heckel, *Remembering Meriwether: White Carolinian Manipulation of the Memory of the Hamburg Massacre of 1876*, a thesis presented to the Graduate School of Clemson University, Clemson, South Carolina, December 2016.

[84] Heckel, *Remembering Meriwether*, 57.

[85] *Edgefield Advertiser*, March 11, 1914.

[86] *Edgefield Advertiser*, February 23, 1916.

[87] Hughes, "Images."

[88] Rosson, *History of North Augusta*, 15–16.

[89] Rosson, 19.

[90] Cashin, *Story*, 210.

[91] Cashin, *Brightest*, 216.

[92] Editorial, *The North Augusta Star*, May 31, 2017.

[93] Cashin, *Story*, 210.

[94] Cashin, *Brightest,* 229, 231.

[95] Don Rhodes, "Exhibit celebrates heyday of Palmetto Park," *Augusta Chronicle*, February14, 2010. https://www.augustachronicle.com/article/20100214/NEWS/302149925; and Don Rhodes, "Real-life Eve of 'Three Faces of Eve' Honored at Funeral," *Augusta Chronicle*, August 3, 2016. https://www.augustachronicle.com/things-do/applause/2016-08-03/ramblin- rhodes-real-life-eve-three-faces-eve-honored-funeral.

[96] Editorial, *The North Augusta Star*, July 8, 2015.

[97] James Folker, "Blacks Killed in 1876 Get Marker," *Augusta Chronicle*, March 7, 2016.

[98] James Folker, "North Augusta Dealing with Monument Issue," *Augusta Chronicle,* September 27, 2017.

[99] Phyllis Britt, "It's Time to Put Racial Animosity Aside," *North Augusta Star*, August 23, 2017.

[100] Robert Pettit, *Report to the City Council of North Augusta: Recommendations Regarding the Meriwether Monument in Calhoun Park,* November 2018.

[101] Cashin, *Story*, 146–47.

INDEX

T

Thankful Baptist Church 180
Thigpen, Corbett H. 180
Thirteenth Street 102, 169, 176
Thomas Green 158
Thompson, Waddy 81
Thomson, John Edgar 101
The Three Faces of Eve 180
Thurmond Lake & Dam 178
Tilden, Samuel 150
Tillman 40, 118, 119, 130, 131, 132,
    133, 134, 141, 143, 144, 145,
    147, 158, 159, 160, 161, 162,
    203, 207
Tillman, Benjamin Ryan 160, 203
Tommy (J.T.) 120, 121, 122, 131, 134,
    137, 153
Tom Thumb 50, 58
Town ix, x, xi, xii, xiii, xiv, xv, xvi,
    xvii, xxi, xxii, 2, 4, 6, 19, 22,
    23, 24, 26, 27, 28, 29, 33, 34,
    35, 37, 38, 39, 40, 42, 43, 44, 45,
    46, 47, 48, 50, 55, 59, 60, 68,
    69, 70, 71, 72, 73, 74, 75, 76, 77,
    80, 81, 82, 84, 85, 86, 88, 93,
    94, 95, 97, 98, 99, 105, 107, 108,
    109, 110, 114, 115, 116, 123,
    124, 126, 127, 132, 134, 135,
    142, 144, 145, 147, 154, 157,
    158, 160, 165, 166, 167, 168,
    169, 170, 171, 172, 173, 174, 175,
    176, 177, 178, 179, 180, 182,
    183, 186, 188, 189, 192, 193,
    194, 196, 197, 199, 200, 202,
    203, 205, 206, 208
tract 15, 24, 34, 37, 39, 41, 42, 46, 47,
    48, 173

U

Union Herald 137
Upper Hamburg xix, 39, 41, 42, 48,
    179, 181, 187
US Lumber Company 185

V

Vandervelde, Isabel 136, 203, 207
Virgo, Lauren xvii, 192
virtual tour xvii, 192, 193
Voight-Lassen, Irene 4, 5, 204, 205

W

Wade, II 145, 146
Walker, William H. T. 195
Washington, George 91, 92, 151
West Point 58, 60, 63, 64, 65, 67
West Point Foundry 58, 60, 63, 65
Winthrop College 159
Woodward, Joanne 180

Y

Yarborough, John W. 87
Young Men's Union Association
    182, 185

Z

Zier, Kelly 190

Printed in the United States
by Baker & Taylor Publisher Services